Hakon of Rogen's Saga

Erik Haugaard

Illustrated by Leo and Diane Dillon

"Far to the north in Norway, where the winter sea has a deep voice and at mid-winter the sun hides its face, lies the island of Rogen. I was born on that island, in the year of the Great Hunger, when only kings and earls slept with filled stomachs . . . Rogen was my father's birthright. For nine generations it had passed from father to son, and no king in his castle had more power than my father had on his island."

So begins this saga of a bleak island whose craggy peaks embrace a little world of its own, of a widowed father who rashly kidnaps an earl's daughter for his new bride, of the vengeance that swiftly follows, of a brother's treachery, of a small boy grown wise beyond his years who survives bloodshed and tragedy to seek his own birthright along with his manhood.

Here is a novel of immense power that perfectly catches the mood of a harsh but heroic people. The sullen forces of evil may beat on Rogen like the swells of the dark northern seas, but like the precious rays of the returning sun, courage, honor and love bring the promise of new life to its sea-swept valleys and meadows.

Erik Haugaard writes: "I have attempted to tell the story of a boy who lived at the end of the Viking period. It was not written for 'youth,' in the sense that I have blunted my pen before I started. I abhor those writers who have not the skill to keep the attention of adults, and therefore think themselves equipped to write for children. I have done my best, and I leave you to be my critic."

author of a play, The Heroes, which first presented at Antioch College in 1958. He, his wife Myrna (also a writer) and their two children live in Denmark.

HAKON OF
ROGEN'S SAGA

HAKON OF ROGEN'S SAGA

ERIK CHRISTIAN
HAUGAARD

Illustrated by Leo and Diane Dillon

HOUGHTON MIFFLIN COMPANY BOSTON
The Riverside Press Cambridge

19929

For my daughter,
MIKKA:
a bribe, that she may
not think
too badly of her
father

PREFACE

—————

YOUR DOG, your horse, your friends, and you, yourself: all shall die. Eternally live only your deeds and man's judgment over them." This was the credo of the Vikings — the lonely heroes ever watched by the future, ever composing their own sagas. From manhood unto death, they were players upon a public stage that stretched from the northern tip of Norway west to Greenland, east to Nizhni-Novgorod, and south to Constantinople, which they called Mikkelgard.

They were not a nation; Norway had more kings than all of the countries of Europe have today. They were a group of poets who, according to their own taste and ability, were composing epic poems out of their lives.

Their gods fitted them: Odin and Thor, father and son, Gods of Battle and Brutality. Freya, the Goddess of Love; and Frig, who guarded the apples from which the gods ate to keep their youth eternally. The Vikings had many gods, for their poems were long and well written. Loki, the God of Evil: the God of the Broken Promise, whose symbol was the fire; and Balder, the God of Goodness, who, swordless, was to inherit the world, when all the other gods had died.

They were not romantic heroes, for the romantic hero is but a dream — a paper doll cut with a pair of embroidery scissors. They were intensely alive; their minds and bodies were linked together, as Achilles' and Hector's were.

In *Hakon of Rogen's Saga*, I have attempted to tell the story of a boy who lived at the end of the Viking period. It was not written for "youth," in the sense that I have blunted my pen before I started. I abhor those writers who have not the skill to keep the attention of adults, and therefore think themselves equipped to write for children. I have done my best, and I leave you to be my critic.

HAKON OF
ROGEN'S SAGA

1

FAR TO THE NORTH in Norway, where the winter sea has a deep voice and at midwinter the sun hides its face, lies the Island of Rogen. I was born on that island, in the year of the Great Hunger, when only kings and earls slept with filled stomachs. My father was Olaf the Lame; my mother Sigurd Hakonsdaughter, who could claim kinship with the mighty Earls of Tronhjem. My mother died giving birth to me, and I was suckled by the slave woman Gunhild who had had a girl child two months before.

A motherless child is both an object of pity and of scorn. He learns early to depend upon himself, for he is hardened by never having experienced the mother's gift to the child, that love which never asks why. Love came to me only as a reward, something which depended upon my own behavior.

Rogen was my father's birthright. For nine generations it had passed from father to son, and no king in his castle had more power than my father had on his island. Nineteen families lived on Rogen, about two hundred human beings, all subjects of my father. In our hall, besides my father and myself, lived four young unmarried men, five women whom the sea or sickness had made husbandless, and seven children, all of whom were fatherless. These were all freemen. My father owned four slaves, who also lived in our house: three men and one woman, Gunhild, who had suckled me.

These slaves were not mistreated, yet absence of liberty is in itself mistreatment. Let those who defend slavery try once, themselves, to be slaves. But these were not the thoughts of my childhood, for a child lives in an expanding world, where tomorrow is an unknown land. Among the slaves was a man named Rark. He was my friend, and gave to me — if not the mother love that I missed — at least the father love that my own father either could not or would not give me.

I believe that my father never forgave me for causing my mother's death. I hardly ever remember him smiling and I never heard him laugh. His world was one of gloom, of evil forebodings, of disasters lurking behind each day like hungry wolves behind trees. His birth present to me was a feeling of guilt, which covered me as a cloud does the mountaintop. My father was not really lame, but his right knee was stiff from an arrow wound that he had received in a battle against the Danes.

Rogen, my childhood kingdom, was not very large measured with the strides of a grownup; but with a child's steps, which never go in a straight line, it was a huge world. To the south and to the north it ended in a mountain. These two mountains were identical in height, but the southern one was peaked, and therefore appeared higher. The top of the northern mountain was a flat plateau.

East of the northern mountain, which was named after Thor, a small peninsula jutted into the sea. This peninsula was low and formed a crescent, like a newly born moon. Here nature had provided us with a harbor, protected on three sides by Rogen itself; and to the south, where it faced the open sea, by a small island, on which the sheep grazed in the summer.

Thor's Mountain was part of our homes; it loomed behind the buildings, shielding us from our worst enemy, the northwest wind. It was easy to climb and had good summer grazing for our cows — a friendly mountain with shrubwood for our fires and hares for our pots.

The southern mountain was steep, difficult to climb, and had poor grazing; its name was the Mountain of the Sun. There were openings in this mountain, entrances to caves inhabited by fairies and elves. It was even told that one of them was the entrance to Hades, the World of the Shadows, where those who do not die in battle go after death. The grownups told tales about the Mountain of the Sun to scare the children into behaving; and we were all terrified of it, especially at night, when sleep had closed our eyes and we were left with only our imaginations to see by.

Between the two mountains was a fertile valley that had good grazing. Here we harvested, in summer, the hay which kept our cattle alive during the winter. Here, too, was located the other village, for there were two on the island. This one was smaller than ours, and there lived only six families in it.

A man could walk from one end of Rogen to the

other in a day, and across it in much less: a little world surrounded by a world of water so huge that only the gods could measure it.

We could not have done without our water world. It gave us the big codfish, with its stupid, bulging eyes; the quick herring, silver-coated; and the seal, that big animal which has the eyes of a dog, breathes like a man, and swims like a fish. We feared the sea and loved it: it fed us and rocked us in our boats, like a mother who rocks a child to sleep in her arms. In summer its little waves laughed as they broke upon the beach; and in winter it shouted, "Stay away! Stay away!" as its fists hammered against the shore. The sea was the road that led to everywhere, and beyond its horizon lay the reality that our dreams were made from.

The lands beyond the sea: in the long winter nights, we listened to tales about them. Each trip that any member of our household had ever taken was relived, and memory gave youth to the old. The slaves told the children stories of their native lands — sad stories, told with a longing heart. My friend Rark was the only one of the slaves who had been captured as an adult; therefore, his stories were especially prized, and thought to be more truthful. He came from a country south-west of ours, so far away that should you start your journey when the moon was full, you would only get there — and then only with fair winds — when it had disappeared from the sky.

Rark had been well connected in his own country; he told me that he had owned far more land there than the Island of Rogen. He brooded much over the fate

4

of his wife and children. When once I remarked to him "But they are wealthy," he explained, "The heart of man is so constructed that greed and envy own it; and pity and love are only guests. Widows and orphans are often better protected by a beggar's cloak than by a fur cape."

My memories of the first five years of my life are but isolated incidents, comparable to lines of unconnected poetry that stand in your mind: at once meaningless and meaningful. I have a picture of myself falling off the wooden pier to which our smaller boats were moored. Who it was that saved me, I do not remember. Other of my memories are mere feelings, vague and disjointed: a series of pearls through which no hole can be drilled, and so, no necklace made.

2

It is hakon, who did it!"

I hid deeper among the bearskins, believing that if I could not see my pursuers, they would not be able to see me — for it was I who had "done it." I had broken one of my father's arrows. This would not have been so serious, if it hadn't been his "lucky arrow"; the arrow he had received as a gift from the Earl of Tronhjem.

"Where is he?"

I heard my father's deep voice, and buried my face in the skins, so that not one ray of light illuminated the darkness I was staring into.

"Come on. Out with you."

I lay motionless under the skins, keeping my eyes closed. Then my cover was torn from me. A hand grabbed me by the ear, and I was brought to a sitting position.

"Get up."

As I rose from the bed, I looked at my father's face, trying to guess the extent of his anger.

"Why did you do it?"

Grownups always seem to know "why," and children hardly ever do. Why had I taken the arrow and played with it? I didn't know. But I did know one thing, and this was that the truth would serve me badly.

"I wanted to use it." Hardly had I spoken these words before I knew that they would not suffice.

"What is the use of an arrow without a bow?"

"Rark was going to make me a bow." This was a half-truth, for though the slave had promised to make me a bow, he had not said when. But my father's anger was already spent. He stared at me, as if I were a stranger; then turned and gazed at Gunhild and the children, who were witnessing my shame.

"Don't touch what doesn't belong to you." He made this statement in a flat, low voice; then, as if he had suddenly remembered that one more action was expected of him to finish the ritual, he raised his arm and struck me a blow with the flat of his hand on my cheek. He did not wait to hear me cry out, but turned on his heel and marched out of the room.

"Why did he hit me?" I was talking to Rark, who was sitting on the little wharf to which the smaller boats were moored.

"Because you had deserved it."

My cheek was still burning from my father's blow. Rark hadn't convinced me. "Maybe I did deserve it, but that wasn't the reason he hit me. I think he did it because the others expected him to."

Rark smiled and changed the subject. "You want me to make you a bow?"

"Yes, I need to learn to shoot."

At this Rark laughed. "Your seventh summer has not yet ended and you think of becoming a warrior."

When I had awakened that morning, I had not given the bow a thought; but now I knew that I wanted it more than anything I had ever wanted before.

"I shall make you one, but first you must ask your father's permission."

"I don't ever want to talk to him again." I knew that these were childish words, and being angry with myself for having said them, I picked up a pebble and threw it out into the sea.

"A slave may not bear weapons. What would your father say if he saw me making a bow and arrows?"

Rark had spoken the truth, and I could not answer him; therefore, I got up and walked toward the house.

"Only a fool does not know that pride makes a poor shield," he called after me.

The great hall was empty except for Helga, the daughter of the slave woman Gunhild. She was sitting playing with a small doll, which Rark had made for her.

"Your father was very angry."

I merely looked at her without saying anything.

"Did it hurt much?"

"No!" I answered, and then added meanly, "What concern is that of yours?"

Helga was a strange child: small of stature, yet not dwarflike or ill-proportioned. Her face was always serious, as if she knew the fate of all of us and, therefore, was willing to forgive us. She and I had been brought up almost as sister and brother; the bond of having suckled at the same breast was stronger than the difference in our positions. Born of a slave, Helga herself was a slave.

I knew that she loved me, and I could hurt her. But I also loved her, and I always ended paying for my behavior with a bad conscience. I could see that tears were forming in her eyes, and I hastened to say, "It did hurt."

She took my remark for what it was, a peace offering. "Is Rark going to make you a bow?"

I nodded.

"Your father has gone to visit Sigurd."

The news made me happy, because it put off until the next day my asking permission for Rark to make the bow. I lay down on one of the beds, which were built along the walls of the hall. Helga sat down at the end of the bed and watched my face. No doubt she was wondering how I would react to the news she was about to give me.

"I think your father is going to Tronhjem."

I stared back at her. "Is Sigurd going with him?"

She nodded.

Neither of us liked Sigurd, my father's younger brother. He bragged and had a sharp tongue. It seemed to give him pleasure to embarrass us children.

"Who else is going?"

Helga glanced around the hall, as though she were afraid of being overheard. "They are taking twenty men. I don't know whom they have selected."

"Why are they going?"

Helga didn't answer, but started stroking my leg. I pulled my leg away from her, and repeated my question.

"They say that your father is going to seek a new

9

wife. They say he is going to ask for the hand of Thora Magnusdaughter."

I wanted to ask who Thora Magnusdaughter might be, but instead I said, "And who are *they* that you got all your information from?"

"My mother heard your father talking with Erik the Poet about it. He told him to get the boats ready."

Before I left the room, I gave Helga's long hair a hard pull. She gave a little scream and called after me, "You are a bad child, Hakon Olafson. I hope your father beats you even harder next time."

I found Erik the Poet in one of the storehouses. He was measuring a piece of new rope. Erik was a big man, bigger and stronger than my father, but he was shy and seldom spoke more than three words in a row. That is why my Uncle Sigurd had nicknamed him Erik the Poet.

"I hear that my father is getting ready to sail for Tronhjem."

Erik contemplated the rope; then glanced at me and nodded, thus saving himself the trouble of saying a word.

"Is it true that he will seek himself a wife in Tronhjem?"

Erik took out a knife and started to cut the rope, never once looking up at me.

"Can't you answer?"

Erik rolled the measured pieces of rope together and then, as he had thrown the coil over his back to carry it down to the ship, he said, "They say it is so."

10

Before I could ask him another question, he was gone. I drifted out into the sunshine, telling myself that it wasn't true; yet I knew all the time that it was.

It was beautiful, the day my father departed. The men rowed the big boat out as far as the tip of Grass Island, and then they hoisted the sail. The wind was westerly. Slowly — the big sail bulging as it rose — the ship leaned over on the summer sea, and started on its trip south to Tronhjem.

One of the last things my father did, before he left, was to give Rark permission to make me a bow. Dreams fly fast and no boy's legs can catch them. I had hoped that I would bring back a bird or a hare, the very first day I went hunting. I set out with ten arrows and came back with seven — one of them, a broken one. Rark laughed at me. But the next day he took me in back of one of the storehouses and drew a circle on the wall. He measured a distance of about five spear-lengths, and there he placed a stone.

"Stand there," he ordered, pointing to the stone. "When four out of five of your arrows hit the mark upon the wall, then the hares on Rogen will have need to hide."

Every morning I practiced, but it took a long time before my arrows flew as I willed. Two months went by, after my first luckless hunt, before I killed a hare. By then, my father had long since returned from Tronhjem — returned without his hoped-for bride.

At first I was relieved. While he had been away, all of the women of the hall had felt sorry for me — and a little for themselves as well. Who was Thora Magnus-daughter? And what kind of mistress would she make? A man may work in the fields and seldom see his chieftain, but the widows and the woman slave Gunhild would be constantly in their mistress's vicinity.

Though my father did not confide in me, he was less taciturn now, and his expression sometimes had a lightness I had never noticed before, which made the other expression, the moments of sadness, more terrible to see.

Three times my father set sail for Tronhjem, his ship laden with gifts; and three times he returned without a bride. The fourth spring — the year I was eleven — he took with him forty men. In our hall, only the old men were left behind; but my Uncle Sigurd, who twice before had sailed with my father, now refused to accompany him, and of all the men of his village only Harold the Bowbender was among my father's companions.

"This time Olaf Sigurdson will return with a bride or he will not return at all." Helga's voice was sharp and mocking, so unlike the way she usually spoke that I knew she was repeating what the older women were saying.

The moon waned and grew whole again before my father returned. One day, when we were sitting, eating the midday meal, one of the other children, a boy named Rolf, came running into the hall and cried, "They are back!"

As soon as we stepped outside the hall, we could see the sail. The ship itself was not visible because Grass Island lay between it and us. Soon the sail was furled, and we could hear the oars splashing in the water. I was frightened and I moved a little away from the others. Suddenly, I felt a hand in mine. It was little Helga; she had come to comfort me. I looked at her and smiled. She returned my smile, and the smiles linked up together, and we felt stronger and less afraid.

"This is Hakon."

I glanced up at the woman who stood before me. Thora Magnusdaughter was beautiful: tall and fair.

"This is your new mother."

I looked from Thora to my father. Something within me rebelled and I ran away.

"Hakon!" my father shouted after me.

Then I heard Thora saying, "Let him be, don't frighten him."

She was wrong. It had not been fear that had made me run away. Your life can be divided into periods. My life would now be divided into those things that had happened before my stepmother arrived and those afterward. This was the beginning of a new period; and it was my realization of this fact that had made me flee. Would the future be good or evil? To this I did not give a thought. I only knew that I stood at the dawn of a new day.

3

Gunhild need not have feared the coming of Thora, for she was like a summer wind, from her came no warning of winter snow; and yet, she would be the cause of many men's deaths. Maybe Rogen is too far north for more than the promise of spring; and maybe the dark winter is its natural garment.

We all knew that as a suitor my father had not been wholly welcome by Magnus Thorsen; else he would have been given his bride long since. Yet he had always been treated politely and each time given hope that soon — perhaps next spring — Magnus would force himself to part with his daughter. Magnus was a widower. Five years before, his two sons had set out on an expedition to Iceland with Knud the Strong, and none of them had ever been heard of again. Thora was the younger of Magnus' two daughters, and he claimed to love her above all else.

When my father arrived in Tronhjem for the fourth time, accompanied by twice as many men as had ever come with him before, Magnus did not invite him to sleep in his hall. My father and his men camped near where their boat had been beached, and Magnus sold them food at winter prices, but my father acted as if he had not noticed these deliberate insults. Finally Magnus invited my father to partake of a meal, but he did not treat him as one should a guest of honor. He seated him at the far end of the long table, next to one of his freemen. Again my father took no notice of the insult. This irritated Magnus, and he started to bait my father.

"Olaf Sigurdson, is it true that where you come from people are so poor that they must live all winter on dried fish?"

"You have lent your ears to slanderous tales," my father replied. "In Rogen we live in winter on hay and the bark of trees. I understand that here in Tronhjem men are fed like babes that have no teeth, and that old women chew their food for them."

Magnus grew pale, for he was a man much older than my father, and had indeed few teeth left in his mouth; and certainly not enough strength in his arms to challenge my father to single combat. "Go with peace, Olaf Sigurdson." Then turning to one of his men, he added, "That it shall not be said that anyone left Magnus Thorsen's house as poor as he came, gave him a chicken to take home with him. He can slaughter it to his gods at the Midwinter Feast."

Magnus believed in the new god, my father in the old. It was customary at the Midwinter Feast to sacrifice an ox to Odin; and therefore the gift of a chicken was an insult not only to my father, but to his god as well.

My father rose, grasping the handle of his sword, he made his way to the door; then he turned swiftly and stared for a moment at the people seated at the table, as if he wanted to remember every face. Then he spoke this verse:

> "The cock crows loud
>   When it is old
>   But iron will rust
>   And blood grow cold."

Without another word, he departed. When he returned to his boat, he gave the order to sail. To any observer — and there were many of Magnus' men about — it appeared as if he were getting ready for the trip to Rogen. He sailed straight out to sea, and while the boat was still visible from land he set the course due north. This was, however, only a ruse to fool Magnus

and his men; once well out of their sight, my father had the sail furled and they rowed for shore.

The boat was beached at a cove that was a fairly long walk from Magnus' hall, and here they waited until evening; then, leaving ten men to guard the boat, my father and thirty men set out to avenge the honor of their gods.

Of the actual fighting at Magnus' hall, I have never heard a believable account. My father never spoke of it, and those of his companions who did, boasted so much — each of his own personal valor — that I would blush to retell their tales.

Magnus escaped, it is said, in his nightshirt. We lost two men: Gudman and Eirik were their names. My father gained a bride, Thora, and the people of Rogen, a powerful enemy, her father.

My father had stolen Thora from her home, but her love had come to him as a gift; for it soon became obvious that Thora was not sorry to dwell among us. And I, for one, was not sorry that she had come. She never tried to become my mother, but treated me as if I were her brother. She confided in me and allowed me to accompany her on her walks. She was fond of walking and of picking flowers; and such was her power that none ever thought of ridiculing her for it.

Gay, my father never could be. The features of his face had been cast by the gods to remind man that life is sad. Yet when he looked into my stepmother's face, his eyes grew soft with longing, and were like two pools that promised sweet water.

The summer passed and the fall fogs came rolling in from the sea like the poisonous breath of the Midgard Worm, which encircles the world. We all knew that, sooner or later, Magnus or one of his kinsmen would visit us to avenge the affronts my father had dealt them. I think that is why we greeted the first western storm with relief rather than the usual curses; for it meant that we were safe. No one dared come near Rogen in winter.

If you stood on top of Thor's Mountain, it would appear as if the whitest of necklaces surrounded the island; but it was no necklace, it was a noose: a breaking, tearing surf that no man — or even god — could swim through.

Already the sun hardly rose before it set; and yet, both the sheep and the cows were still fat, for the summer had been kind and we had had a good harvest.

The winter passed with work. Old weapons were repaired and new ones made, clothes were woven by the women, and wool was carded and spun. Yet this winter was different from any I had ever known before. Thora with the shy eyes and the slow smile won my love, and I followed her like a puppy. My Uncle Sigurd jested of it once, saying that my father should fear me as a rival. My father only smiled and said, "Oh, Thora has enough love for both me and my son." And then he caressed my hair. This was the first time I can remember my father showing that he loved me. Even now, many years after, I still seem to feel his hand; and for a moment, through my memory, he lives.

Unpleasant things happened, as well, that winter. Three of our best cows fell ill and died; and in the village where my Uncle Sigurd lived, one of the storehouses burned, causing my uncle great losses, since it was there that most of the wool from that summer had been stored.

At the Midwinter Feast my father and my Uncle Sigurd became angry at each other and almost fought. During the festivities all of the inhabitants of the island were my father's guests; but it was customary on Rogen that the wealthier men bring along with them a gift of a sheep or a cow, for the feast lasted many days, and even the slaves ate nothing but meat. My Uncle Sigurd brought nothing, in spite of his being, next to my father, the wealthiest man among us. My father did not remark upon this, though I could see on his face, when he greeted his brother, that it ill-pleased him, for Sigurd had brought thirty mouths, besides his own to feed.

At last there were no more bull calves or oxen to kill, and my father gave orders to his men to butcher a cow. That evening when the meal was served, my uncle commented upon the meat, saying that it was tasty and good for the jaws. Then he looked at the men who had done the butchering, and asked them if they had won the race or if the cow had managed to beat them by dying of old age before her throat was cut.

My father turned pale. The cow's meat had not been served at the main table, but at the table where the servants, widows, and slaves ate.

"If my younger brother has lost his teeth, let him eat with the old women."

This time it was my uncle's turn to blanch. "I at least do not endanger the lives of my friends for the sake of my appetite." My uncle was referring to the fact that my father had made so many enemies for us, by robbing Magnus Thorsen of his daughter.

My father jumped up, upsetting his drinking horn and spilling his mead out over the table. It was not customary at the Midwinter Feast to wear weapons at table, so his hand searched in vain for his sword.

It was Thora who calmed my father. "A jest must be treated as a jest," she said; then looking at my uncle she added, "A coward counts danger in his bed, as a miser does his silver."

My father smiled, for it was well known that my uncle was not brave and many a time, when challenged to a duel, he had bought his life with silver.

My uncle said nothing; but he returned the next day with his men to his village, there to brood over the insult and in the dark winter night think up suitable replies. The hate of brother against brother runs deep, for their lives are bound together by common memories: a rope which is as strong as the one the gods used when they tied the Fenris Wolf.

4

Spring came early the following year. In March all the snow in the meadows had melted, and from the top of Thor's Mountain hundreds of little brooks played their way to the sea. On Grass Island the gulls started building their nests and screaming their silly cry of defiance to the world. Only the birds of prey, the falcon and the eagle, are more beautiful in flight than the seagull; but when the gull lands, it shows that it has a slave's soul. Each type of gull — and there were three kinds on Grass Island — lives apart like separate tribes. And like tribes they fight, and even at the height of the herring season there never seems to be fish enough for their greedy little eyes. Greedy they are! A gull will drop a fish from his bill, in order to swoop down on some weaker gull to steal his fish. Like men they live in colonies, and like us they spend their days in arguments and squabbles. When a gull is ill and can no longer fly, the other gulls kill it.

I have sometimes wondered if this were an offering. Do gulls have gods as we do? In the old times, men were offered to Odin and Thor. Who was sacrificed to the gods: the strong? or the weak, the broken-winged?

I have asked some of the old people, but none of them was old enough to have ever seen a man sacrificed.

The only enemies that the gull has, besides nature, are themselves and, in the spring, human beings. Gull eggs taste as good as their bodies do foul. Egg-hunting was the duty of the women and the children, and no duty was ever performed with lighter hearts.

One day, when the sun shone so warmly that one had to look at the snow-covered peaks of the mountains, to remind oneself that it was not summer, my stepmother asked me to take her to Grass Island. We rowed over in one of the small boats. The wind blew gently from the south and the tiniest of waves played against the hull. Seen from the sea, the view of the hall, and all the other buildings surrounding it, was beautiful. My stepmother sighed as she looked at it, and her features looked so sad that I could not help asking, "Why do you sigh?"

She gazed at me for a moment, and then, averting her eyes, she looked into the sea. "I am afraid, Hakon."

I was busy rowing the boat and having trouble keeping it on its course.

"My father," she continued, "is a mighty man. He can destroy your father."

I smiled at her and said, "But you are happy here."

She laughed, as if I had told a joke. "It was my father's pride, not his heart, that was hurt when your father stole me away. He will come to avenge himself; or — what is worse — send my cousin, Rolf Blackbeard."

At that moment the boat reached the island. We leaped ashore. Thora spoke no more of her father or her fears, and I was so young that I soon forgot our conversation in the excitement of the egg-hunt.

We had come a little too early. Not many of the nests had eggs in them, and this made the suspense of the hunt greater. In the high season, each nest will yield four or five eggs, and you can pick a basketful without walking more than a hundred steps. But that day we scoured the length and breadth of the island, and returned to our boat with only one small basketful of eggs.

By the end of April, the snow had melted on Thor's Mountain, and only on the very peak of the Mountain of the Sun were a few white spots still visible. My father, being well aware of the dangerous enemies he had made, sent two young men to the southern tip of Rogen, to set up camp there for the summer. They were to act as sentries, and send us warning if they sighted any ships.

On top of Thor's Mountain, my father decided to construct a house that could be used as a retreat should Magnus Thorsen come with a force so large that we could not defend our villages. The walls of this building were constructed from stones found on or near the plateau, which formed the top of the mountain. Their measurements were identical with the measurements of our largest storehouse. This was done because we did not have the time or the lumber to build a new roof for our mountain fortress. We took the roof from the storehouse and transported it, piece by piece, to the top

24

of the mountain, where it was assembled again, to become the roof of the new house.

There were several paths to the peak of Thor's Mountain, but they all met, like so many brooks, a hundred steps from the top. Here, where the paths joined, my father built a wall that formed a semicircle, running from one impassable part of the mountain to the other. The wall was two hundred steps long, and so high that a grown man could just see over it. My father's idea was to bring the whole population of Rogen to the top of the mountain. Weapons, clothing, food, pots and other utensils for cooking were carried up to the new storehouse; then we gathered and piled huge quantities of wood for our fires.

In all this work, neither my uncle nor any of his men took part. He visited our fortress once and commented that it had a very fine view. My father, who was present, ignored him, and went on with his work as if the words had never been spoken. My uncle made one remark, though, which was valuable: he pointed out that there was no water on the plateau.

When my uncle was about to leave, my father at last spoke to him. "Will you and your men come, when I send for you?"

My uncle looked out over the sea, toward the mainland; I think he feared that his eyes might give the lie to his words. "Only a coward would sit on his hands, when a kinsman cried for help."

My father looked at him suspiciously, probably remembering that his brother had refused to accompany him on his last trip to Tronhjem.

We soon found that no well could be dug on the peak of Thor's Mountain. All the holes we made ended in sheer rock, at the depth of a man's waist.

At one corner of the plateau, the stone showed through the grass, and the earth was no deeper than a finger's length. Here we stripped the earth from an area fifteen steps long and ten steps wide, and in the center of it we made a shallow basin to hold rain water. This was very slow work, and many tools were broken while doing it. The first rainfall filled the basin up, and it appeared like a small lake — a very small one to supply drinking water for so many people.

Spring passed and summer came. On Grass Island the eggs hatched, and the gulls were busy filling their young ones' stomachs with fish. When at Midsummer, Magnus Thorsen and his men had not yet arrived, we grew lighthearted; and the young men pretended to be sorry that they would get no chance to prove their courage.

But unfortunately for many of them, their courage would be tested that summer, and many a jestful lip would scream its death cry before it had learned to form the words of love. One evening, as we sat at table, a young man pushed the door to the hall open with such force that the door banged against the wall.

We all turned to look at him, while he stood in the doorway trying to catch his breath. His head was wet with sweat, and his face white, for he had run all the way from the south of the island.

"They are coming!"

Oh, he needn't have said it. We all knew his message before it was spoken.

"One ship?" My father's hand held a bone upon which, a moment before, he had been gnawing; now it was poised halfway between the table and his mouth, as he waited for an answer.

"Three ships."

My father dropped the bone. It fell clattering, first onto the table, then to the floor, where it was immediately grasped by a dog's jaws.

If I had not known, I could have guessed how serious this news was by the way my father slumped together in his seat. For a moment he looked like an old man. "Are they big ships?" he almost whispered.

"There are at least a hundred men in each."

In the silence the words, although they had not been spoken loudly, sounded like the noise of thunder. We had, at most, seventy men of weapon-bearing age on the island: four swords to one would be our lot.

My father stood up. "Victories are given by the gods!"

No one looked at him, but an old man whispered, "And defeat is the gift of your enemies."

"Bring out some mead, and let each man drink to our victory!" The mead was brought and the drinking horns filled. Then my father spoke this verse:

> "A man's name
> Never dies,
> Eternal fame
> In courage lies."

Lifting his horn toward the sky, he shouted, "To the gods! To victory!"

The men regained their spirit and the blood that Magnus' men soon would spill surged through their veins, shouting life and courage.

All the old men, women, and children were sent to our fortress. They were to drive along with them two cows and a herd of sheep. These, and the five pigs which had already been transported to the plateau, and some dried fish were to be our food supply.

The wind blew from the north, and Magnus' ships could not use their sails; therefore, their progress against the waves was slow. We would have all night to prepare ourselves for their attack. Our fortress was strong, and our desperation made us cunning and resourceful.

5

I WAS SENT on horseback to summon my uncle and his men to come to our aid. There were only three horses on Rogen — two that belonged to my father and a stallion that was the property of my uncle. I rode the small mare. She was a pretty animal: brownish black in color and of a docile temperament. I felt very grown-up, being the bearer of such a message. I was thinking of putting it into verse, as was the custom of the adults when they spoke of matters of importance.

When I entered my uncle's hall, I found him and his men still at table.

"They have come!"

I had expected these words to have the effect of a sudden wind that springs up on a calm day, and in a moment whips the sea white. But my uncle did not even glance at me. He continued gnawing on the rib of a pig, as if I had spoken about the arrival of a school of fish.

"My father has sent me to ask you to come!"

My uncle only smiled.

"You will come?" I believe that I knew the answer before I had asked the question.

My uncle laughed, and told me to remember these lines of verse, so I could repeat them to my father:

"No mouse grows fat
That fights
A hungry cat.
Nor will night
Become day,
Because a fool
Will have his way."

Anger filled me as suddenly as a pitcher is filled in a deep well; and as the water spills over the pitcher's rim, so did my anger. "An ill-made verse, like soggy wood, will kindle no fire. Go tell him yourself, if you dare!"

Some of the men laughed and my uncle's face darkened with rage. "A pup that barks when the sun rises will whine before it sets."

I turned from my uncle, and looked from one to the other of his men. "Will no one come?"

They avoided my eyes, and none of them rose. Then, in anger, I spoke my first lines of verse:

"Sigurd will hide,
Swordless his side,
Coward his name,
Infamy his fame."

As I walked out of the hall, three men got up to follow me: Harold the Bowbender, who had been with my father on his every trip to Tronhjem, and his two sons.

"Hakon!" Harold called after me, as I got up on my horse. "Wait and we will come with you."

I was pleased, for they were the best warriors in my uncle's village; but I could not wait for them, because I had to hasten to my father to tell him the news of Sigurd's treachery. Harold and his sons promised to come as soon as they had gathered their weapons. I dug my heels into the sides of the mare and galloped homeward.

Along the way I met two old men who were taking the remainder of the sheep and cows south, to the Mountain of the Sun. I told them of my uncle's betrayal, and they decided to drive the animals across the island, and then south, in order to bypass his hall.

I admitted that I did not think well of the whole idea. Surely our enemies would find the animals. Would it not be better to slaughter them and throw them into the sea?

"And what would we eat this winter?" one of the old men said. And I am certain he added in his mind, You little fool.

I did not argue with them.

The animals struggled up a steep hill, protesting wildly, not understanding why they could not follow their usual paths. I knew every one of these animals by name. Could I really have killed them and dumped their bodies into the sea? I rode on. In the distance I heard the bleating of the sheep — a sound of home, of comfort, of peace.

When I arrived back at the hall, I could see that my

father had given up hope of giving battle there. The inside of the hall was stripped of everything valuable; it appeared as if it had been raided. The floor was littered with worn-out skins and clothing, and no fire was burning in the hearth.

I was told that my father was down at the harbor. Twenty men — among them my father — were pulling the big boat up on land. When they saw me, they paused in their work. "What news do you bring, Hakon?"

I looked down at my feet, trying to think of a way to phrase my news. "He is not coming," I blurted.

For the second time that day my father looked to me as if he were an old man. He muttered a verse, but he did not look at us. Instead he gazed at the sky, as if he were speaking to the gods:

> "Loki's gift:
> Envy and greed;
> Sand to sift,
> Snakes to breed."

Then — as at the table when he had heard of the approach of Magnus' ships — he straightened his back, as if his worries were burdens that he could throw off like a sack.

"Let the ship be!" he ordered.

"Aren't we going to burn it?" one of the young men asked in surprise.

"If we win, we shall sail in it again. If not, it will not matter. Let no man call Olaf Sigurdson mean or ungenerous, even to his enemies." My father smiled, a small bitter smile, and walked back to the hall. The men and I followed him, but none dared walk beside him.

The last things were packed and carried up to our fortress; and yet, my father tarried. I think he wanted to say goodbye. I believe he knew that he would never return. He didn't seem to be aware that I had stayed behind with him. He walked about the hall, his eyes searching and yet blind. For a moment, he stood at the hearth and scuffed the dead ashes; then, as though an idea had occurred to him, he walked to the door, only to stand there, looking back into the hall. Slowly he turned and walked outside. The stillness of the hall shouted in my ears and I fled.

From the doorway I could see my father. He was making his way, slowly, down to the ship. I followed him hesitantly, like a dog that is not sure whether or not it ought to have a bad conscience.

He walked around the boat. He stood by the prow, his hand caressing the wood. Though his eyes were gazing out over the sea, he called to me. I walked up to him, both flattered and frightened.

"I had hoped one day to sail with you." A forlorn smile curved his lips: a smile without gaiety.

"We will win, Father!" I was not a man yet, and lived still in a world where the brave killed giants without difficulty.

"I sacrificed our last bull to Odin, while you were gone." Then he sighed and paused. "I think the gods have died. I know that it is said that this would not happen before the end of the world; but maybe the

new god that the King believes in has killed them."
Then, he spoke this verse:

> "Thor's hammer will fall
> And Odin grow blind,
> Deserted Freya's Hall
> And tearless the wind."

We both stood motionless for a long time — or what seemed to me a long time. Suddenly we heard, from far away, the voices of men and the noise of oars in the water. We returned to the hall. From there, we could see out over Grass Island to the sea beyond it. The three ships were beautiful, and so calm was the water near the island that their reflection was almost as real as they were.

"There are more than three hundred men," he said softly. "Come, my son, let us go to our men."

The compliment my father paid me by saying "our men" made my feet light and my heart easy; for death is a shadow that the eyes of a child cannot see.

6

THE WIND blew from the east and carried the voices of the invaders up to us on the mountain. We watched them take possession of our homes, and knew by the rising smoke from the hole in the roof above the hearth that the fires had been lit again. We were so near our homes that we could see everything; and yet, so far away that most of us despaired of ever living in them again.

As Thora had feared, it was not Magnus Thorsen who led the invaders, but his nephew, Rolf Blackbeard, renowned for his ability with a sword and his courage. But courage without pity and feeling is mere brutality, and deserves even more contempt than cowardliness does.

Magnus had stayed at home, telling anyone in Tronhjem who cared to listen to him that my father was a common robber and it was beneath his dignity to punish him personally. An agreement might have been reached with Magnus, for he was fond of gold and probably would have found a price for his honor. Rolf was cruel. He found pleasure in playing with his victims. He was a cat, not a bear. My stepmother, Thora, hated him; for her heart bled for the weak who like sticks of wood are caught in the surf, those lowly ones whose death no one desires to avenge.

The first few days, the invaders did not come near our mountain fortress. They were busy planning their attack. They sent scouts to spy on us, but they were careful to keep at a distance, beyond the reach of an arrow.

Each day that spared us from battle weakened our spirit. We watched the water diminish in our lake, and it seemed to me that our courage sank with it. In all the stories of ancient times that I had ever heard during the long winter nights, the hero was fearless, he went into battle as lighthearted as if he were attending a feast. Were all these stories lies, or were they just dreams? In a hunchback's dream, no back is crooked. Still, I believe I know now what courage is: it is to smile, when fear has locked all smiles within your breast.

A week passed without any battle. We wounded one of their scouts, and they, one of our sentries. But in order for our losses to be equal we should have wounded four of their men, for we were but seventy and they were more than three hundred.

On Odin's Day, ten days after their arrival, the enemy attacked in force.

On the morning of that hideous day, a thick fog came up from the south. Beginning on the sea, it had crawled over the island and up the mountainside, until it covered our camp. We could see nothing; but almost worse was the fact that we could not hear. The voice of a person standing nearby sounded as if it came from a great distance.

Our sentries did not see their attackers before they were upon them. They screamed for help, but the fog made it difficult for us to guess from what direction the screams came.

Though the fog gave the enemy an initial advantage, it proved no friend to them either. For we fought on land that we knew, while they were fighting on strange soil, and often we heard their curses as they stumbled upon the rocks. It was a strange battle. An approaching shadow might be an enemy or a friend, and more than one man killed his comrade, that day.

"To the ships! To the ships!" This loud cry, as if shouted by a giant, rent its way through the fog, and all men stood still.

"For Odin! For Odin!" This time it was my father's voice, and it felt as if cold water were trickling down our spines.

"To the ships!" our enemies now screamed.

"For Odin!" we answered, as loud as we could.

The enemy retreated down the side of the mountain. The sun broke through the fog and tore it asunder, leaving the mountaintop bare in the noonday sun. For a moment we stood in silence, then the screams, curses, and moans of the wounded began. This is the song of the battlefield that no one dares tell.

Twelve of our comrades were shooting arrows in Odin's company, and another six were wounded so seriously that we feared for their lives as well. Eighteen subtracted from seventy leaves fifty-two; but

when my father counted us, he only reached the number forty-eight. Four of our men were missing. Had they been captured, or had they fled? We did not know; but when we heard their names, many of us suspected that they had used their legs to better purpose than their arms.

How many of the enemy did we send to their new god? We found twenty-three dead and fourteen wounded. A victory! How hollow are these words, for over death there is no victory.

"Did you kill anyone, Hakon?" asked an old man who had sailed with my grandfather when he followed the King to fight the Danes.

"I don't know," I answered and stared at my sword.

"Is there any blood on it?"

I took the blade in my hands, to examine it more carefully. The old man laughed. Yes, there was blood. Had I killed a man, or only wounded him? My stomach grew tight, like a rock inside me. "Kill," so short a word for so big and terrible a deed.

I walked away, to the farthest edge of the plateau. I did not want to talk, I wanted to think. Far beneath me, I saw the island stretching out to the sea. That ever-moving sea! And it struck me as a terrible injustice that if tomorrow all of us were killed the sea would break with the same monotonous beat upon the shore. I was growing up. But how painful is the process, and how doubtful the profit!

"Hakon."

I turned angrily, not wanting my self-pity interrupted. It was Helga. On the tip of my tongue was a sharp word, but the tears in Helga's eyes stopped it. I smiled, and she threw herself down beside me and buried her head in my lap.

"I was afraid, so terribly afraid!" she cried.

I smoothed down her hair and murmured, "Little sister . . . little sister."

She had been locked in the storehouse with the other children and the women. In the dark room they had sat; the children crying from fear and the women with fear-filled faces comforting them. Once a man had banged on the door and demanded to be let in. A moment later, they had heard his death scream. When the door finally opened and they saw a friend's face — and not an unknown enemy — peering into the darkness, they had run out into the blinding sun, like so many bats.

"Will they sail away now?" Helga asked, pointing toward the harbor.

"Sail away!" I almost shouted. "Do you think that Rolf Blackbeard is defeated so easily?"

"But they shouted 'To the ships!' "

"Oh, that," I returned with contempt. "That was just the Viking command for retreat . . . But they will come again."

"Next time, don't let them lock me in the house," she pleaded.

I smiled at her, but made no promise, knowing full well that I would not be able to keep it.

"Will they kill Father Olaf?" It was Helga's habit

always to refer to my father as "Father Olaf." Her mother scolded her for it, but I think it pleased my father.

For the moment, I forgot Helga. I was thinking of my father. For the first time it struck me that he, too, had once been twelve years old. I do not know why the thought comforted me, and why a tear ran out of my eye and down my cheek.

7

AFTER the battle, the men of Rogen claimed that it was the god Thor who had shouted "To the ships!" in order to confuse the enemy; and many swore that they had seen him fighting on our side. I knew better, for I had recognized the voice. It had been Rark, the slave, who had saved us. For saved us he had; if the battle had continued until the fog lifted, we would all have been killed. But tomorrow, would the gods help us then? For the victory we had won was merely a breathing spell between battles; and indeed we needed the help of Thor.

I thought it an injustice that no one should know of Rark's heroism, and I went in search of my father. I found him and my stepmother sitting on the parapet. My father was gazing down at our enemies. "They will come again, soon." His voice was serious; yet his expression was not glum, and he placed his hand tenderly on Thora's shoulder.

When my stepmother saw me, she said gaily, "Here comes our brave little warrior."

"What do you want, Hakon?" my father asked.

As always in my father's presence, I fumbled for words. "It was Rark," I finally blurted.

He looked at me quizzically. "What was Rark?"

"I mean . . . I mean, that it was Rark, not Thor, who shouted 'To the ships!' "

My father jumped down from the wall and, smiling bitterly, he muttered, "Oh, I knew it wasn't the gods."

Something was wrong. Somehow, I hadn't explained it well. I had expected my father to be happy and proud of Rark, and instead he seemed so hopelessly sad. "I thought you should know . . . He fought very bravely," I mumbled.

Again my father smiled that bitter smile, from which all mirth is absent. "No slave shall fight for Olaf Sigurdson. Go and tell Rark he is a free man."

Agilely, Thora had leaped down from the parapet; and now, as I was about to go away, she put her arm around me and pulled me close to her. "Let me go to my cousin Rolf and beg for our lives," she pleaded.

"A man of honor does not beg," my father whispered.

"But it is *I* who will beg. A woman does not mind begging, for she can give birth to life and knows how precious it is." Then she let me go and, lowering her voice, as if she were telling a secret, she added, "Love carries its own pride, and it is often mistaken for humbleness."

"Hakon." My father and my stepmother were standing close together, and I suddenly realized that they were the same height — and I had always thought that my father was the taller. "Tell Rark to come here. I want to talk with him."

"Rark, my father wants to talk with you."

Rark was sitting on the ground repairing an arrow. He did not look up at me, but continued wrapping the leather thong around the shaft, where it had been cleft. "Did you tell him?" he asked softly.

"Yes," I answered, "and he wants to thank you. He said you are a free man."

"It would have been better for all if I had remained a slave a little longer."

"I don't . . . I don't really understand," I complained unhappily.

Rark patted my head. "Fear is natural to man, and courage a kind of blindness. If your father truly believed — as the other men do — that the gods were fighting on his side, we might win — even against odds like ours."

Now I understood my father's bitter smile. Oh, how crooked is the course that man must sail!

"My son tells me that it is you, we must thank for our lives."

Rark looked at the ground.

"Thor," my father called mockingly, and Rark lifted his head and stared at him. This time it was my father who found need of observing the color of the earth. "I cannot even give you your freedom, for I have left among my treasures only death. But you may tell anyone you meet that you have saved Olaf of Rogen's life, and that he called you brother."

They both stood silent now, looking into each other's faces without shame.

"I shall not forget the duty of a brother," said Rark.

My father laughed ironically. "Trust only the brothers of your choosing. Those the gods give to you may be the gift of Loki, rather than Thor. Remember not your duty to me, but your duty to yourself as a man, and I shall not fare badly from your deeds."

When Rark and I were alone he asked me, "Hakon, what is one's duty to oneself?"

I might have been able to reply years later, but then I was only twelve years old, and had only phrases learned from others with which to answer such questions. "It is one's duty to defend one's honor," I said a little uncertainly.

"Is it one's duty to love?"

I looked at him blankly. How should I know? I who had only known child love, which is like a little brook; how could I from its shallow turbulence, imagine a river?

The wounded prisoners were sent to join their friends, for we had not food and water enough, even for ourselves. My father told one of the wounded men to deliver a message to Rolf Blackbeard: to tell him that he would meet Rolf in single combat to decide the victory.

From a safe distance, an answer was soon shouted back to us, "Rolf Thorson does not fight in single combat with a robber!"

Thora grew very angry when she heard this; and swiftly she climbed up on the parapet. "Tell Rolf, that scurvious wolf," she screamed to the messenger, "tell him that he is not worthy of serving as a slave to the meanest man in Norway. Tell him that I curse his mother, my aunt, for giving him birth." And then her voice dropped to a whisper. "Tell him that I love my husband . . . that I love . . ." Her voice broke and she almost fell from the stone wall, but my father caught her and lifted her gently down.

Tears were running down Thora's face. My father wiped them away; then, with a sudden movement, he placed his tear-wet hand inside his tunic, near his heart, and said, "I shall keep them there, together with your smiles."

Our enemies gave us two days of peace; then on the morning of the third day, after the first battle, the final struggle began.

It was a clear day. The sun shone on the blue sea and reflected on the shields of the army that was marching up the mountain to fight against us. This time only the children and the old women were locked with the wounded in the storehouse. The young women, the old men, and even two of the wounded bore arms. My father stood on a big rock. From there he spoke to the men:

"The Gods love the brave,
Take them from the grave,
The heroes they call
To live in Odin's hall."

"For Odin! For Thor!" All shouted the words

after my father, though I heard an old man mumble, "For my life."

The enemy was approaching, yelling as they came. I was standing near my father and my stepmother. She looked at me thoughtfully; then she leaned toward my father and whispered something. My father called Rark and another man to him, and before I was aware of what was happening, Rark had grabbed me and lifted me from the ground. The other man took hold of my legs, and, followed by much laughter, I was carried to the storehouse and thrown inside.

I cried tears of humiliation, and cursed kind Rark and my stepmother, who would save my life at the ex-

pense of my pride. In the dark, I heard the whimper of the children, and the moans of the wounded. Then, from outside came shouts and the sound of sword upon sword. The battle had begun.

8

Now it was my turn to have the same experience as little Helga had had. Noise of the battle, screams of the wounded and the dying, and the sound of the clashing of swords and shields came muffled into our darkened world. Nor was our own world silent. One wounded man kept moaning and asking for water; another, who had a high fever, sang a monotonous song over and over again. The most unbearable was a little child who wailed, "Mother . . . Mother . . . Mother . . ." in a voice so filled with despair and hopelessness that one did not feel pity, but anger. Toward a need that one is powerless to fulfill, anger is a common reaction; and many voices cursed that poor little child, who was only repeating an age-old prayer.

I stayed by the door with my sword drawn, for I had decided that if we lost, and an enemy opened the door, I would kill him. As my eyes grew accustomed to the darkness, I began to recognize my fellow prisoners. "Helga," I called just above a whisper.

"Hakon!" She was standing near me, behind an oak beam that supported the roof.

"They have put me with the children," I said bitterly.

"I am glad," she said. To remove the sting she added, "I worried about you last time."

I laid my sword upon the floor and we sat down beside each other. We did not speak, but listened, with our hands clasped, to the battle.

All of a sudden, the noise ceased. It was the custom while two chieftains fought to stop the battle. "If my father kills Rolf Blackbeard . . ." I did not finish my thought. A loud cry came from outside. I jumped up, grabbing my sword. We could hear people talking in excited voices.

"What has happened?" Helga cried.

The door swung open. The glare of the summer sun blinded us. I lifted my sword.

"Hakon," said the soft voice of Magnus Thorsen's daughter, and my sword fell to my side. I looked at her and saw the answer to my question in her tear-stained face.

"Where?" I whispered.

Behind Thora stood a group of the invaders. Now they moved aside and I saw the outstretched figure; Rark was beside it.

"Father!" I screamed but he would never hear me or anyone else again. His face looked peacefully up at me. As I knelt near his head, a butterfly landed on his chest, polished its feelers, and flew away.

"Come." I felt a hand on my shoulder. I rose, obeying the voice of my stepmother.

"Your father was a brave man," someone said kindly.

I nodded. But in my mind, I could not help but ask: And what has his bravery won him?

A few feet away from my father's lay another body. It was the corpse of Rolf Blackbeard. I noticed that the wind made his long, silky beard move, and it appeared as if he were mumbling. "Who won?" I asked.

"No one," answered my stepmother.

"Thora Magnusdaughter," a stern voice interrupted, "in the name of your father, I claim victory."

With scorn Thora turned toward the speaker — a tall, blond man, whose clothes showed that poverty was not a guest in his house.

"It is not my father but his gold that has bought your sword, Ulv Erikson. Let's call my father's gold the victor, or your — and your companions' — greed."

"Claim what you will, Thora, but spare your breath for your father." Then he turned to the men, and ordered Rolf's body to be carried to his ship.

We had been defeated, and the fact that Rolf Blackbeard was among the dead did not alter this fact. Of the hundred and forty-three people who had been on the plateau on the day of the first attack, only seventy-seven did not have scars to show. In the second battle four women had been wounded, and fourteen were dead; of the men, there were twenty-nine wounded and nineteen dead. The enemy had seventy-six dead and eighteen wounded. Also in Tronhjem women would weep.

I sat on the edge of the plateau, wondering what had caused all this grief: My father's love? Magnus Thorsen's pride and greed? (For he had hoped to marry Thora to the Earl of Viken.) So much death. So much pain. And through the years to come, there would be more tears, when memory would give life to the dead.

All of our possessions were taken from us: gold, weapons, anything of value — even the clothes which we wore on feast days were counted among the spoils that Ulv Erikson demanded. Only ourselves, he could not touch; for a Norseman could not make another Norseman his slave. But our own slaves passed to the victors as their property. Gunhild cried when Ulv claimed her as part of his share; for Ulv Erikson had another name, Ulv Hunger. This he was called by his servants and slaves because they were ill-fed.

Ulv wanted Rark as well; Rark had disappeared, together with little Helga, and though they searched long for them, the enemy did not find them.

The day after the battle the dead were buried. A mass grave was dug, and — except for the chieftains — the dead of both sides were left to sleep together like brothers. Rolf Blackbeard's body was to be taken back to Tronhjem, and my father was buried on top of Thor's Mountain. Three shields were placed on top of two of the oars from his boat to make a litter; then a bearskin was thrown over the shields; and on this — his last bed — he was carried by six of his men to his grave. Thora and I walked together — she, for the last time — to the top of Thor's Mountain.

The grave was not very deep, and when my father was lowered into it, Thora fell on her knees, and the tips of her fingers caressed his face. Harold the Bow-bender spoke; but I do not remember what he said, for I was crying the bitter tears of an orphan.

On the way down the mountain, Thora's hand was

in mine. My stepmother was, in reality, Ulv's prisoner, and though he treated her with great courtesy, she could not influence him in any way.

"I wish you could come with me, Hakon," she said. "But I do not know my own future, my father is a harsh man." She grew silent, and I pressed her hand to show that I understood, and did not think that she was abandoning me.

My uncle had not come to my father's burial. He and his men had stayed in their village; and there they had been left in peace. This was the enemy's reward for my uncle's treason. And I began to wonder if, when the invaders were gone, my uncle would not claim my birthright and try to make himself master of Rogen. In one of the stories that the old men told, a fourteen-year-old king had led armies; but I knew that the grown men of Rogen would not take orders from a twelve-year-old boy.

Food for the winter: that too, would be a problem. The enemy had readily found our cattle and sheep wandering on the Mountain of the Sun, and slaughtered them. Some said that my uncle had come to Rolf Blackbeard the day he landed, and told him where our livestock was, in order to save his own.

All this I brooded upon, while the enemy loaded their ships. At times I felt it would be better to beg them to take me along; but my pride would not allow me to beg for mercy from my father's murderers.

Their boats, with our possessions as cargo, lay low in the water. I wished a storm might wreck them; but then, I remembered my stepmother and prayed to Thor that the boat that carried her would reach Tronhjem safely. Ulv credited to his generosity that he did not burn our houses and our boats; but I noticed that my stepmother no longer wore the heavy gold armband that my father had given to her the day she came to Rogen, and I guessed that it was Ulv's greed, not his generosity, that had saved our homes.

It was difficult saying goodbye to Thora: my step-mother, my big sister, my companion of so many walks. "Remember me," she said as we parted. Oh, Thora! As long as I live, a part of you shall live in me! When I saw her figure standing on Ulv Hunger's ship, I realized that she was my first love. Oh, do not laugh! Go and ask your grandfather who was his first love; and when he answers, "your grandmother," ask him again. He will smile, for such is the pain of first love that it leaves no bitterness behind.

South the dark red sails carried them. The wind came from the north and blew fair for them. But what tempest was waiting to rip my sail, to break my slender mast?

9

THE SONG of the sea is always pleasant to the ear; only
the shipwrecked or the starving fisherman will curse
it, as the storm-whipped ocean laughs at his misery.
From my childhood on, it has ever been my friend, I
have listened to its gay song in summer, and my heart
has followed its beat when the winds have whipped it to
anger in the fall storms. The song of the sea is nature's
greatest song. It is, I believe, the voices of the gods,
for in the laughter of the sea, there are hidden tears,
and in its anger, laughter. The bird's song in spring
has no promise of winter in its melody; and the cry
of the seagull in winter, no promise of spring. Only
the voice of the sea says "I am eternal. I am eternal."
And that blessing makes it laugh when the hot sun fon-
dles it, and that curse makes it sigh when the storm-
torn, white moon of winter kisses it.

At dawn — while we were still sleeping — the day
after the enemy had left, my uncle and his men came.
They were all armed, and my uncle was on horseback.
Sigurd Sigurdson flung open the door with such force
that it banged against the wall, awakening all of us.

With sleep-matted eyes we stared at him. He was
wearing his finest clothes and his right hand rested on

his sword hilt. "Awake and dress yourselves," he cried, assuming what he must have thought to be a masterful pose.

"You are late, Sigurd," one of my father's old comrades spoke from his bench. "We are tired from work. We have earned a bit of sleep. Go sing your song somewhere else."

My uncle had little courage but much pride. He drew his sword and walked over to Bjorn, who was lying motionless on his bench, as if he intended to return to sleep. "Get up, Bjorn."

Bjorn smiled and said, "I think I hear a fly buzzing, a carrion fly."

"I warned you!" screamed my uncle, his face contorted with anger. Then swiftly, before anyone could stop him, he thrust his sword through Bjorn.

"Brave man," Bjorn muttered; then sighing, he spoke his last words, "Now I shall sleep." Blood flowed from his mouth, and his body twisted and fell with a dull thud from his bench to the floor.

Rogen that had first been ruled by my father's justice, and later by my stepmother's love, now would know how it felt to be ruled by the sword. Like many weak people's, my uncle's cruelty was dictated by his fears. Ruled by fear himself, he could not conceive that man could be governed by love and respect. Several of the men in the hall gladly would have killed him, but behind him stood his men with swords drawn.

We were a sad-looking group that stood outside the hall in the yellow light of the early autumn morning.

My uncle climbed back upon his horse, feeling no doubt that he could impress us more, speaking from that position.

"My brother harvested the crop that grows from the seeds of folly. The gods have meant people to be ruled, and have given them kings and earls and chieftains to obey. My brother thought himself mightier than Magnus Thorsen and paid the price of disobedience, as Bjorn has just paid it."

Some men mumbled something about not being slaves, but none dared to speak aloud.

"I am now the ruler of Rogen, and those who serve me well shall be fittingly rewarded. And so" — here my uncle laughed — "shall those who serve me ill."

To our surprise, two of Sigurd's men now entered the hall and came back with the body of Bjorn.

"For those who disobey me, there will be shame, and their death shall be like the death of an animal." Turning to his men he ordered, "Go, throw his body into the sea, and let the fishes eat it."

I thought the murder of Bjorn a shameful deed, but his last resting place not an unfit one for a hero.

Each of us had to swear allegiance to Sigurd. When my turn came, my uncle said, "I need not the word of a child. I shall be in your father's stead, and I shall teach you humility. Go among the women, and give me that sword."

I would have rushed at him, but Harold the Bowbender took my sword from me, and whispered in my ear, "The wind cannot break a blade of grass, but it can fell an oak."

I believe that my uncle was disappointed when I did not attack him; for if I had, he could have killed me in self-defense, and no one could ever have disputed his right to my father's property.

My uncle decided to make his home in my father's house. His own he gave to Eirik the Fox, one of his companions: a lying, deceitful man who knew well that his power depended upon my uncle's goodwill. The men whom my uncle suspected of not being loyal to him were divided between the two houses. Two of my father's old friends disappeared shortly afterwards; my uncle claimed that they had been drowned while fishing, but others thought that they had been murdered. With their death the last hope of an open revolt was gone. Backs were bent under the whip of the despot, the weak taking pleasure in it, the strong growing sullen and dull.

Rark and little Helga reappeared. They had been hiding in a cave in the Mountain of the Sun. But Rark, whom my father even before he made him a freeman had treated almost as if he were one, now learned the wages of slavery. All heavy work fell to him, and curses and kicks were his only rewards. The man who lives in the present and has no plans for the future will sink in his own misery, but there are those who will ever invent hope when only despair is present. I knew that Rark was planning his escape, although he did not speak of it, fearing — no doubt — that although my ears were old enough for his secrets my tongue might not be.

Also I learned to work, woman's work: lighting and

tending the fires, scrubbing pots, turning the spit the meat was roasted on. My bow and arrows were taken from me, as my sword had been; even the little knife my father had given me the summer I was six, I was not allowed to keep. My uncle wanted me to appear like a slave to the other men. The clothes I wore were the meanest rags, my sleeping place, among the children. With many of the men he succeeded. Some of them took a pleasure in ordering me — their former chieftain's son — to do the work of a slave. The drink of a slave is bitter water; but from that, too, there is a lesson to be learned. Those who abuse slaves have themselves slaves' souls. They are so foolish that they cannot see the difference between the respect given by a freeman to another freeman and the fawning flattery of a slave. They fill their purses with pebbles and think themselves rich. Foolborn, they strut around like geese in the farmyard, who think their fate will be better than that of the hens.

Little Helga suffered even more than I did from my father's defeat. Used to kindness from my father, and love from her mother, Gunhild, she was doubly robbed. Helga was given to Eirik the Fox to be his slave. Although my uncle was mean, his ambitions were too great for him to spend much of his time tyrannizing a child; but Eirik the Fox was not above such pettiness.

How did Helga bear his mistreatment? She never cried, even when he beat her, but her face grew older, and it was strange to see this little child with the face of an old woman.

All this I was told by the other children, for I saw

Helga only once during that first winter after my father's death. My uncle suspected me of plotting against him and did not allow me to walk far from the hall. The one time I did meet Helga was on a wet, dismal fall day. We were both gathering brushwood on the side of Thor's Mountain.

When I saw how thin she had grown, tears came into my eyes; and when she saw my rags, she wept. "Oh, Hakon, Father Olaf has left us!"

I touched her dirty, matted hair (Eirik had taken her comb from her, and he did not even allow her to wash). "Little Helga . . . little sister, I shall take care of you."

She shook her head and looked down at the ground; and at that moment, the idea that had been so vague in my mind became a certainty.

"We shall run away!" I exclaimed, and pointed out toward the sea. "We shall sail away. We will steal a boat next summer — you, Rark, and me."

When I mentioned Rark's name, a little smile flew over her face; and in that moment it became a child's face again. "They will be expecting me soon, and if I haven't gathered enough wood, Eirik will beat me."

I took all my wood and gave it to her. The heavy bundle on her back made her look like a dwarf, like one of the ones that lives in the mountains. "I will die if you leave without me," she whispered earnestly.

"I shall never leave alone. I swear it!"

She took a few steps. Then she turned around to stare at me. Without another word, a moment later, she was running down the mountainside.

Now I had no wood for myself, and probably would be scolded and made to appear the fool by Sigurd's wife, who was now mistress of my father's hall. But all concern about my own situation had vanished from my mind. I decided that instead of gathering wood, I would climb to the top of the mountain to visit my father's grave.

The wind blew a fierce dance on the plateau. I ran into the storehouse, but it was roofless now and gave little protection. My father's grave had been covered with big boulders. I kneeled by its side, and my blue lips murmured, "I shall avenge you, Father." It was not Magnus Thorsen that I was thinking about when I spoke of vengeance, but my Uncle Sigurd.

A gull screamed near my head. It startled me and I thought that it might be one of Odin's ravens, until I saw its white wings. I glanced up into the cloud-filled sky and spoke loudly: "By Odin, by Thor, I shall avenge myself!"

The winds blew my words out over the sea, and no one heard them; but then, most words spoken to the gods are merely conversations we hold with ourselves.

The day after my visit to my father's grave, I was feverish, and by night I was unconscious. I shivered with cold, though my body was burning like fire under the bearskin that covered me. Had it not been for Rark, I would have died before the Midwinter Feast. He fed me when my hand was too helpless to hold a bowl, and sat by my side during the long nights, when the fever brought monsters to my dreams.

10

WINTER came late that year. It arrived at the time of the Midwinter Feast and, like a hungry guest, it did not like to depart. We learned that year that the bark of trees could be eaten, and there was no animal — no matter how small — that was not hunted. We grew gaunt and our bellies swelled, and the least bit of work made us tired. Seven people died that winter, and we were hardly able to dig their graves. How I survived, who had been sick all fall, must have been by the grace of the gods.

Rark had fed me seaweed, which the others had refused to eat. But I think there must have been magic in it, for, in spring when so many were sick, Rark and I were not. Maybe this is the food of the God of Fishes. Some say that there is a god who has a castle on the bottom of the sea — so far down that the light of the sun doesn't reach it.

Finally spring came, and the sound of a thousand streams were heard again on Rogen. Nature rose from its winter bed and the song of tomorrow began. Each little blade popping up from the ground declared that it soon would be a flower. Even the gulls sang of love, though their voices did not grow any sweeter from it.

Spring green, tender green, stood on the sides of Thor's Mountain, and all the bushes and shrubtrees were sap-swelled, bending complacently to the southern winds and saying, "We knew you would come. We knew you would come."

Most of the human beings on Rogen were too weak to welcome spring. They had gone past hope and despair, and the newborn sun found their eyes a poor place for reflecting its strength. Thanks to Rark, I felt much better than the others, and the coming warmth made me more determined than ever to escape. If we were not able to flee that summer, we would have to spend another winter on Rogen. And would I survive that long? My Uncle Sigurd's face was not a pleasant place to read my future. So many foul deeds had my uncle committed that my murder would not weigh heavily on his conscience.

At present I felt safe, for the battle of survival was not won, and a hungry man thinks more about food than revenge. Of animals, only two horses — my father's mare and a stallion — had survived our hunger.

As soon as the ice on the fjords in Norway had broken and floated out to sea, my uncle set sail for a village called Odin's Cove. Rark and I were ordered to sail with him. It took us five days to reach Odin's Cove — although it was common to do the trip in two — because we were only fourteen men and we could not row the big boat against the waves.

The chieftain of the village, a man named Lief the Lonesome, gave us a friendly welcome. Lief was the only surviving son of Bjorn the Tall, who had been famous for his ability with a sword and for his quick temper. Lief was a peaceful man, having learned from the example of his father that the sword is a poor judge of a grievance.

My uncle bought three pigs, two calves, and a young bull, beside ten yearling sheep and four cows. He paid for the livestock with two gold rings and some silver armbands. I noticed that one of the rings was one he used to wear on his finger, but the others I had never seen before. I realized that they must have constituted part of his private treasure, and recalled with bitterness how the invaders had stripped my father's hall.

We did not stay more than a few days in Odin's Cove. On the second day, we feasted on one of the pigs that my uncle had bought. This was the first time in many months that any of us had had as much to eat as he wanted. Several of the men were too greedy, and they paid for their greed with a painful night.

For Rark the voyage was an ordeal. My uncle tied him to the mast while we were in Odin's Cove. The men grumbled about it, for most of them liked Rark, and several knew that my father had given him his freedom.

This was my first trip, and though the world outside was not that much different from the one I knew, there was enough for me to wonder at. The mountains rose much higher than on Rogen and, for the first time, I saw full-grown trees. I was treated most kindly by Lief the Lonesome, and while the rest of the men ate near the boat, he invited me, as well as my uncle, to sit at his table. This did not please Sigurd Sigurdson, and when

Lief praised my father, my uncle's eyes dwelled upon me with such hatred that I could not look at him. The thought of running away occurred to me. But then I thought of Rark bound to the mast — it would not be an easy task to free him. At night all the men slept on the boats and we would be heard. By daylight any attempt would undoubtedly be seen. There was always someone down by the boats, if not one of Sigurd's men, then one of his host's. Ships are to men, as infants are to women, they cannot pass one by without examining it — one eye filled with tenderness, the other looking sharply, ready to criticize.

Even if I could free Rark, where would we go? To

us this was an unknown land. Certainly the people of Odin's Cove would not help us, for they did not know what kind of man my Uncle Sigurd was.

Lief the Lonesome asked my uncle if I was to be chieftain of Rogen when I came of an age to shoulder such a task. Lief had four daughters, and a marriage into our family would not have displeased him.

Suddenly, in the midst of this conversation, I remembered little Helga — how I had considered escaping without giving her a thought — and my cheeks grew red with shame.

My uncle had two sons, whom I have not as yet mentioned because they were very young. I suspected that he was thinking of them when he replied to Lief's question. "Rogen is Hakon's birthright. He is the oldest — and only son — of my older brother. If it is the gods' will that he shall live to be a man, then Rogen will be his."

Lief smiled at me and said, "Oh, Hakon is a strong lad."

Now my uncle turned to me. While the ghost of a smile — which did not have laughter as a mother — played around his lips, he answered, "Against the will of the gods, none of us can protect ourselves."

The loading of the animals was difficult, especially the bull and the ram gave us trouble. With their legs tied and their eyes turned in protest against the heavens, they mooed and mayed at us from midship during most of the journey. On the return voyage we had lucky winds, and were home in two days.

One of the sheep had broken its leg during the trip. It was slaughtered and its meat roasted. It was not much meat for so many people, and even with the smoked ham that my uncle had received as a gift from Lief the Lonesome, few left the table with filled stomachs. But to the people of Rogen it was a feast. I noticed with disgust that many looked at my uncle with gratitude and admiration, as though the gift of the food had showed him to be their natural leader. Those who had been abroad jested and told tall tales of the feasts we had had in Odin's Cove.

We had milk again for the children, and to make cheese. Three of the cows were excellent milkers, but the fourth had something the matter with its udder: its milk dried up. My uncle had it slaughtered and the meat divided among the households.

My uncle had also managed to buy onions from Lief the Lonesome. It was our luck that the people of Odin's Cove had had a good harvest the year before, for few people can boast of being able to sell onions in the spring. All men who stay at sea for more than a few days must eat a large raw onion daily, or their stomachs will bloat and their gums bleed. Finally, their teeth will fall out, leaving them as ugly as Loki's wife. Many on Rogen had had these complaints that winter and spring; even the women had felt the sailors' sickness. The only two who totally escaped were Rark and myself.

As spring glided into summer, and food was no longer the subject of everyone's conversation, my uncle's plans for me became more and more apparent. In the horror of that winter, the seed of murder had lain dormant in my uncle's mind. He spoke to everyone of my foolishness, and pretended to pity me for not having inherited my father's intelligence. He spoke well of my father and ill of me, and soon some forgot how Sigurd had betrayed his brother. A bird in the hand is worth two in the bush — my uncle had the power and I the birthright. Legal rights are very much like the birds in the bush.

There were a few men on Rogen whom I trusted, but to ask them to help me was the same as to ask them to die. One of them, Erik Longbeard, suggested that I offer to share the island with my uncle.

I retorted angrily, "The only part of my birthright that Sigurd Sigurdson is willing to give me is a plot of land beside my father's grave on Thor's Mountain!"

11

I WAS SURPRISED and suspicious when my uncle, who had taken all my weapons from me, gave me back my bow and quiver of arrows and suggested that I should go hunting. Still, the pleasure of a day away from the hall was too attractive to be spurned, and I set out for the Mountain of the Sun, hoping that I might see little Helga along the way. I did not go directly to the other hall (the one which used to be my uncle's home), because I had no wish to meet Eirik the Fox — between us no love was lost. But in my search for Helga I passed very near the outer buildings, which surrounded the hall. Helga was nowhere to be seen, but a man who was busy mending a fence greeted me by my name, Hakon Olafson, and I took this to be a good omen. It was a sign of respect, for Sigurd and his men never called me anything but Hakon the Orphan.

To be alone in nature, to be an animal among other animals, to feel the sun baking on your back and smell the earth and the grass. I forgot the past and had no thought for the future. I was the first man on earth, ageless as the gods.

I wanted to find the cave that Rark and Helga had hidden in when they had been hunted by Ulv Erikson.

Rark had described it to me. It was located halfway up the southwestern slope of the Mountain of the Sun. Its entrance was narrow, almost blocked by a large boulder. Near the boulder grew two small birch trees.

There are many boulders and many birch trees on the Mountain of the Sun, and it was late, when I finally found the cave. The dark opening was so narrow that I had to squeeze myself through, but once inside, the cave was huge — as big as my father's hall, if not bigger.

The light was very dim, but near the entrance, under some branches, I found a bow and some arrows and a sword. Rark had told me that he had hidden these weapons in the cave. The sword was a fine one. It had belonged to Thorkild the Mute, who had been killed by Ulv Erikson.

A cave attracts and repels you at the same time. It is an opening into the unknown: into a sunless and moonless world, where you might meet your most bitter dreams.

There are often deep holes in the floor of a cave. I had no fire, and I did not dare to explore it without light.

On the way home I hunted for hares, but my luck was not with me. By the foot of the Mountain of the Sun, I hid among some bushes, hoping that the hares would be tempted by the good grazing in front of my hiding place.

No hares came. It was growing late. The shadow of the mountain stretched out over the valley, and the evening breeze was chilly. I stood up, and at that moment, I realized that I was not the only hunter on the Mountain of the Sun that day. An arrow sang past my ear. I threw myself upon the ground, expecting a second arrow to follow the first, but none came. I looked towards the mountain, for the arrow had come from behind, but I could see no one. I leaped over the bushes and threw myself down along the other side of them, so that I would be protected from the view of my hunter. For, that I was the hare for whom that arrow had been intended, I did not doubt. A little less than an arrow's shot above me, a pile of boulders made a perfect shelter for a hunter. I put an arrow in my bow and pointed it in that direction.

How long I lay clutching the bent bow, I do not know, but my hands began to tremble. Finally, when the ache in my arms became unbearable, I turned my gaze away from the boulders and, to my amazement, saw the hunter.

It was Eirik the Fox. He had retreated from the boulders by following a dried out riverbed. He was now below me. He must have thought that I had fled, when I jumped over the bushes, for he was walking confidently, making no effort to conceal himself.

Not far away I found the arrow that had missed me. The arrow told me nothing; it could have been anyone's arrow. I put it in my quiver — that arrow that had destroyed my childhood world. I looked at my shadow — the only companion that I dared trust — and laughed.

On the way back, a thousand plans occurred to me, but none satisfied me. When I entered the hall I found

my uncle seated at the table with Eirik. They both looked up and Eirik scowled.

"Well, Hakon, how many hares do you bring us?" My uncle's voice was jovial, but his face stern.

"None . . . I saw a fox though. If it had been within arrow's shot I would have killed it."

Neither my uncle nor Eirik responded. I placed my weapons at my sleeping place; then, taking Eirik's arrow from the quiver, I walked back to the table. "I found an arrow: an ill-made arrow, a crooked arrow, an arrow like the one Loki killed the God Balder with." I threw the arrow down in front of them, and kept my glance on Eirik's face.

"Where did you find it?" my uncle asked.

"It came flying like a bird — like a crow."

My uncle took the arrow into his hands and, breaking it in two, he said, "Yes, it is an ill-made arrow." He rose and flung the broken arrow into the fire and watched it burn. "And you are an ill-natured boy."

At my uncle's words, a shiver passed through me and I knew that I had been a vain fool. We were not alone in the hall. Sigurd's wife, Signe, a stupid woman who worshipped her husband as a dog its master, was stirring the soup kettle, which hung over the hearth.

"Pack your things," my uncle ordered. "You are to go with Eirik and stay at his house."

"So long as my father's house stands, I need not work for strangers."

In a few quick strides, my uncle crossed that part of the hall that separated us. His arm was lifted and his hand clenched.

I knew what was to come, but I did not stir. The

fifth time my uncle hit me, I fell to the ground and a loud scream opened my tightly closed lips. Blood ran from my nose and mouth. It tasted salty, like the waters of the sea. Twice my uncle kicked me, then my memory stopped. My last thought was, "Now I die."

I did not die. Some of the men had come when they heard my screams and this saved me. My side ached and my nose swelled to almost double its normal size; but in a few days I was up and around again.

If I breathed deeply, it felt as though a knife were being stuck in my side, and I could lift nothing. My uncle acted as if I didn't exist, and I knew that he was making plans for my murder. I was too weak to attempt to escape; besides, there was my promise to little Helga. All I could do to save myself was to keep close to the hall and to other people.

Seven days after my beating, my aunt told me to go to Thor's Mountain to gather wood. I went to my sleeping place to get my bow and arrows, but she took them from me saying, "I told you to gather wood, not to hunt."

I thought of appealing to her, but she was not clever enough to respect the rights of any but the strong. Besides, the thought of what her sons would inherit, if I were killed, made her a willing accomplice to my murder, though I doubt if she herself could have delivered the death blow.

As I looked at Thor's Mountain from the yard in front of the hall, it struck me as being as good a place as any to die. I was so tired, so weak. The yard was empty, for all the men had been sent out to fish. I looked about me and whispered, "I shall never see this again." Here I had played when a child. A cat came out of one of the storehouses, blinked its eyes at the sun, and sat down to wash itself. Tears of self-pity formed in my eyes and rolled down my cheeks. It is hard to die, especially when you are only thirteen years old.

As I passed one of the haystacks, a pebble hit me on my shoulder. I turned and there was Rark. He beckoned me to come. I ran to obey him, my heart beating with new-found hope at the sight of his face.

"Your uncle and Eirik the Fox, with three of his men, are on Thor's Mountain. They are going to kill you."

I nodded wearily.

"Go to the cave."

Again I nodded.

Rark took me by the shoulders and shook me gently. "Hakon, are you a child that a beating can break you?"

I could not explain to him that it was not the beating, for, to be perfectly truthful, I did not know what had broken my spirit.

"I have a plan. I shall come to you soon. Be brave, little Hakon."

My uncle's blows had not made me weep, but Rark's kindness did. When he called me "little Hakon," the tears came running like a spring rain. Rark let me cry, holding me close to him without speaking.

When my tears had finally stopped, I felt much better, and Rark laughed. "Will you go to the cave?"

"Yes," I answered firmly and, turning my face defiantly toward Thor's Mountain, I decided that it was too early to hunt for my grave.

"You will need a fire and some skins. Stay here by the haystack, until I come back."

I sat down on the ground at a spot where the haystack would protect me from view, both from the hall and the mountain. The spirit of life, which so mysteriously had been drained from me, came back now like a tide. The idea of living alone in a cave in the Mountain of the Sun appealed to me. It seemed to be the pleasantest house a boy of thirteen could have.

When Rark returned, he had with him a bearskin and a clay pot, filled with embers and ashes. From one ear of the pot to the other, he had tied a piece of rope, so that I could carry it without burning my hands.

"Now run, Hakon. But don't build too large a fire."

I threw the bearskin over my back and picked up the pot. When I turned to say goodbye to Rark, he had disappeared. I took the path which followed the sea until I was near Eirik's hall, then I crossed the island, thinking it better to approach the mountain from the more deserted, western shore.

It was almost midnight when I came to the cave. The sun had disappeared under the horizon, but a strong red glow burned over the dark sea. I entered my cave and built a fire. The flames' flickering light illuminated the cave's high loft. It was a huge cave and even now, at Midsummer, very cold. I wrapped myself in the bearskin and fell asleep. I dreamed about my father and Thora; but my father had Rark's features, and Thora's face was tear stained.

12

If you have learned to be alone without fear, then no man can call you weak, though your arms be unfit to wield a sword or an axe. Many a strong man trembles when night has made him a small island in the ocean of darkness and the hooting owl is heard. But the man who is hunted learns that the most lonely place is the friendliest and that night is better than day.

When I awoke from my first sleep in my new home, I was thirsty. The fire had burned down; in the gray ashes only a few red embers glowed. I rekindled the fire, but kept it burning low, for fear that the smoke, which streamed out of the small crevice in the rocks above the entrance, might lead my enemies to the cave. I took my bow and arrows and the earthen pot, and went in search of a spring.

The Mountain of the Sun was much more barren than Thor's Mountain; little soil clung to its sides, and the trees were hardly more than bushes. I was long in finding a spring of clear water. My hunter's luck, however, was with me.

In a tiny valley, I saw two hares busy eating. They were not as frightened as the hares that live near the halls, and I was very close to them before I shot my arrow. One of the hares was pierced in the neck and died instantly, leaping only once and then lying still. The other hare looked with surprise at its comrade, but did not run away as I had expected.

Quickly I took a second arrow from my quiver, and shot again. Being excited, my aim was faulty, and instead of hitting the forepart of the animal, my arrow lodged itself in one of the rear legs. With an arrow protruding from its leg, and blood trailing it, the hare ran away.

I had only four arrows. The loss of one was serious to me; but more than this, I did not like the thought of the wounded animal dying a painful and slow death. I spent the rest of the day trailing the poor hare. Finally, I found it. The arrow had gotten caught between two branches, and the animal, having only one thought — to push forward — was trapped. A second arrow killed it, and I returned to the cave.

I cleaned both hares and skinned one of them; its rear leg I pierced with a stick and broiled over the fire. The meat of the freshly killed hare is tough; it should hang several days before it is fit for a meal. But hunger made my teeth sharp.

What concerned me most was that the spring was so far away, for my little pot could not hold a day's ration of water; but I gave no more than a few moments thought to this problem before I was deeply asleep.

My fire and bedding lay near the opening of the cave. How far back the cave stretched, I did not know, but I was determined to find out. The next morning I

gathered more wood and built a second fire farther
back. From its light I could see that, by an ever-
narrowing passage, the cave went deeper and deeper
into the mountain.

Returning to the entrance for more wood, I noticed
that it was less smoky there than where my fire was.
Excitedly I realized that this meant that there must be
another exit to the cave for the smoke to disappear
through.

The wood was not dry enough to make decent
torches. I had only walked a few steps when the flames
died. I crawled to what I judged to be the end of the
cave and built a third fire there. At this point the loft

of the cave was just above my head, and the smoke made my eyes water, but the mystery of where the smoke went was solved. In the light of the flames I saw a large hole — big enough for me to attempt to crawl into it. But the smoke was too heavy — my eyes were smarting. I retreated from the cave, out into the fresh air.

I thought I might find a second entrance to my cave farther up the mountain, but I looked in vain for signs of smoke from the fires. Far below me stretched the never-ending sea; looking down at it, I saw a small beach. I did not know that there were any beaches on the southern shore of Rogen. The white sand gleamed friendlily up at me, and I started to climb down the mountain forgetting my search for the smoke. But very soon the mountainside became too steep, and I grew frightened of falling. I was keeping my eyes on the beach — trying to find the best way to descend — when my feet no longer had rock beneath them. I had fallen into a hole. It was not very deep and I was more frightened than hurt.

The hole was as deep as I was tall, and my nose-tip was level with the ground. I had lost my bow and quiver of arrows in the fall. The bow I found lying at my feet, at the bottom of the hole. As I bent down to pick it up, I smelled smoke!

The rock that formed the floor of the hole was filled with small crevices — the largest being so big that I could push my hand through it — and out of all of these was pouring smoke. I had hoped to find a second entrance that I could use to escape through, should my uncle and his men discover the cave. This exit could only be of use to a lizard. Disappointed, I climbed out of the hole.

I looked for my arrows near the place where I had stumbled but, to my surprise, they were not to be seen. The mountain fell sharply away at this point, and carefully, lying on my stomach, I leaned over the edge. Below me, hanging from the branches of a small bush, was my quiver of arrows. The distance was no greater than I could have jumped, had the plateau not been so tiny that I feared falling over the edge.

Without my arrows I would starve, so necessity made me choiceless. Grabbing hold of a protruding rock with both my hands, I slowly edged my body over the side of the mountain. When I had lowered myself as far as my arms could stretch, I let go and fell!

When my feet hit the ground, I bent my knees and fell forward. Except for a scraped knee I was unhurt, and there, facing me, was the second entrance to my cave! A large gaping hollow in the mountain!

That it was an opening to my cave, there was no doubt, for I could smell smoke. I had to bend my head to enter, but once inside, I could stand upright.

It was a small cave and from the innermost part of it a tunnel led into the mountain. I started crawling. The first reaches were well-lighted. From the tiny openings that I had discovered in the bottom of the hole into which I had fallen such a short time before, shafts of sharp light played upon the floor. I climbed on, upward and deeper into the mountain. Soon my body blocked the lights from the tiny crevices and the darkest of nights engulfed me.

Several times I bumped my head. The roof of the tunnel became so low that I had to squeeze myself through like a snake. I crawled on and on blindly — my hands were now my eyes. I was frightened and tired, my breath came in short gasps, and had the tunnel been wide enough for me to turn around, I probably would have.

The passage was becoming narrower and narrower, and there was smoke. What if it weren't the smoke from my own fire I was smelling? In the mountains live the dwarfs. They were Odin's friends, but were they mine? I called Odin's name but no one answered. The tunnel curved slightly. I flung my hand above my head. I touched nothing. Forward, my arm could reach freely in all directions. I saw two eyes of fire staring at me. I gave a cry of fear!

Was this the cave where the Fenris Wolf was tied? And were those his eyes I was staring into? I buried my head in my hands and dared not look up, while I kept saying, "Odin! Odin! Odin!"

Only stillness greeted my cries. I lifted my head. The eyes were still there, but now there were not two, but many. I scrambled forward, my fear gone. The eyes of the Fenris Wolf were the brilliant embers from my fire. I was back in the big cave. I ran to the entrance and out into the sunlight.

I had been only a short time inside the mountain, but now I understood the horror of Hades — of that shadow world for those who do not die in battle.

Soon the passage between the two caves became very

familiar to me. I moved all my belongings into the smaller cave, since it was safer and less frightening.

I quickly discovered that it was a short climb from the plateau to the beach and, halfway down, I found a spring. The beach itself served me with as much drift-wood for my fire as I could use. The hearth in the new cave was my special pride. I built my fire in the back of the cave and the smoke passed through the tunnel and out of the small crevices. Even the biggest of fires caused no tears to come to my eyes, and should anyone find the big cave and discover the passage, they would have to pass through the smoke-filled tunnel and jump over my fire, in order to reach me. I was contented and proud of myself, but soon the wish to see Rark overcame me, and I started to plan a nocturnal visit to my uncle's hall.

13

I PLANNED to visit my uncle during the night, that is to say, during that part of our summer day when the sun for a short time withdraws its face beneath the horizon. As day and night become one in common darkness at midwinter, so does day reign uninterrupted over Rogen in summer. Winter is night and black; summer is day and white. Still, man must sleep. We are not like bears, who can hunt all summer and sleep all winter.

I left the cave while the sun was still above the horizon, walking along the western and most deserted shore of the island. When I reached the foothills of Thor's Mountain, the sun had set. The low clouds that hung over the sea were on fire; the sky above was not blue, but white. I was armed only with my bow and arrows. Rark's sword was too long and heavy for me to have taken it along.

I had decided to approach the hall from Thor's Mountain instead of from the sea, because to make one's way from the water's edge to the house, at any hour, was to risk being seen. I believe men's hearts must belong to the sea for, whether they wish to be consoled in their grief or have their happiness enhanced, they walk to its shore.

I sat down and rested. I needed many things. I had only two arrows left and the scantiest of rags for clothing. But, first and foremost, I had come in order to find Rark. In the winter he usually slept in the cowshed, but in summer he often slept outside. Before me lay the woods, "the forest" as we called it — though there was not a tree that was taller than a full-grown man. Between the forest and the house stretched a meadow where the cows grazed; the sheep, who were not allowed there in summer, were given the poorer grazing farther inland. I walked through the forest to the edge of the meadow. Now I could clearly see a thin streak of blue smoke coming from the opening in the roof of the hall. I waited in the shadow of the trees until I was certain that no guard had been posted, then I darted forth and ran across the meadow, not stopping until I reached the haystack where I had seen Rark last. I had had an idea that he might be sleeping there, but he was not. Next I searched the cowshed and the smaller storehouses.

The entrance to the large storehouse was directly opposite the entrance to the hall, and I was afraid that someone might hear me when I opened the door. The storehouse was empty, or almost empty, for in the corner were some sheepskins, rope, and ship's tackle.

I was just about to leave, when I heard a noise outside the door. I hesitated and then ran towards the sheepskins, burying myself among them. My hiding place had a most unpleasant smell, for the skins had not been cured.

The door opened and I heard my uncle say, "A flea will make a giant scratch."

Eirik the Fox's voice was high like a woman's, and a shiver ran down my back when I recognized it. "When you want to catch a wolf, you tie a lamb to a pole and hide nearby."

"Maybe he is already dead." But I was sure from the tone of my uncle's voice that he did not believe his own words.

"Why should he be?" Eirik was quarrelsome.

"What is your plan?" My uncle's feigned indifference was obviously an attempt to guard his purse.

"The slave girl Helga, whom you gave me as a present, we will send to the Mountain of the Sun —"

My uncle interrupted Eirik. "I didn't give you the girl."

A curse flew from Eirik's lips, and then some words I could not hear, but they must have angered my uncle, for he said threateningly, "Few men keep a fox as a pet. Beware Eirik!"

When Eirik spoke again, his tone was as humble as his words. "Sigurd Sigurdson, I have sworn to serve you, and so I shall. All that I own is yours."

"Then what is your plan? Be quick. It is getting chilly."

"My plan . . ." Here Eirik paused, as though he had wanted to say something else and then thought better of it. "My plan is to post men on the Mountain of the Sun and send Helga to gather wood there. When

Hakon sees her, he will come out, and we shall catch him."

"I don't want him alive. I want him dead."

What madness is it, that makes a man want power, that makes him wish to rule others with such passion, that he will sacrifice all his virtues to achieve it?

"You have my permission to try your plan. And if you bring me his head, I shall reward you for it." With these words my uncle left the storehouse. Eirik followed him and closed the door behind them.

I stuck my head out from under the skins. I was nearly suffocating from the smell. With my fingers I touched my face and, for a moment, I saw my own head being exchanged for a gold ring.

My uncle's mentioning that he had felt chilly made me certain that he had returned to the hall, but where had Eirik gone? I opened the door cautiously and peeped out. No one seemed to be about. Quickly I flung the door open and dived round the storehouse and out of sight of the hall.

My heart was beating so loudly in my breast that it seemed to echo in my ears. A dog started to bark. It was my father's dog Trold. (It was my luck that most of the dogs had died during the winter, usually we had ten or more dogs around the hall.) Trold came up to me, wagging his tail, much more pleased to see me than I was to see him. I scratched him behind the ears and he whined gently with pleasure, his tail banging against the wall of the house behind which I was hiding.

I realized that I would have to give up trying to find

Rark; it was too dangerous. There seemed nothing else for me to do but return to my cave. No one saw me run across the meadow except a lone cow, that with a loud *moo* greeted me as I ran past. Trold had followed me and would not return to the hall; now I was pleased to have his company.

Taking the same path back along the western shore that I had followed on the way out, I thought about my situation. I would have to free little Helga as soon as possible, for I feared that if Eirik the Fox's first plan failed, he might get the idea of torturing little Helga to make me do something rash. Suddenly it struck me that perhaps this was a good time to visit Eirik's hall. I crossed the island to the south of my destination and then turned north.

Surrounding the beach close by Eirik's hall were large boulders, which made very fine hiding places. I ran from behind one to behind another, until I was near enough to the buildings to see if anybody was about. There were seven buildings in all: two halls — the largest being the one my uncle had given to Eirik — and five storage houses. There was no one in sight. Somewhere in one of these silent buildings little Helga slept, but to try to discover which one might be to risk my life.

Drawn up on the narrow beach was an eight-oared boat. It was almost new; the oars and the mast were in it, but not the sails. I put my shoulder to the side of the boat, but I could not budge it. Inside it were some fishing lines and hooks, and these I took. There was also a smaller boat anchored by a big rock, in the shallow water.

Suddenly, I heard Trold growl. I glanced up toward the buildings, taking an arrow from my quiver at the same time. A man was coming out of Eirik's hall. I threw myself to the ground alongside the boat.

It was Harold the Bowbender. He looked up at the sky and then out over the sea. I watched him. He had been a friend to my father, and had been along on that unhappy trip to Tronhjem. I remembered too that he had followed me out of the hall, on that terrible day when I had brought the message to my Uncle Sigurd of the invaders coming, and that he and his sons were the only ones among my uncle's men who had fought to defend Rogen. Harold was now walking down toward the boat. He was unarmed.

With my hand I muzzled Trold, fearing that he would bark. Harold didn't see me, though he passed only a few steps away. Leaning against the other side of the beached boat, he stood motionless, contemplating the sea. I rose and drew the bowstring tight, then, pointing the arrow at his back, I spoke:

> "The tide of luck
>   Ran out to sea,
>   The hammer struck
>   But killed not me."

Harold looked at me with such wonder in his face, that I could not help smiling. Then he answered:

"The grave will speak
Where a strong man lies,
Only the weak
With his fortune dies."

I lowered my bow, and he took me in his arms and embraced me, as is the custom among friends.

We talked much, and I told Harold about the conversation I had overheard between Eirik the Fox and my uncle. Harold promised that he would protect little Helga, and that he would — if need be — die for my cause. With Harold, his two sons, Rark, and myself, there were enough of us to handle one of the smaller boats and escape from the island. Harold brought me some clothes, gave me ten more arrows and a pair of shoes. I returned to the cave, where I roasted some hare, and Trold and I had a feast.

14

Tomorrow, that for so long had meant added fear, now was a word of comfort to me. So foolish was my uncle's and Eirik's rule over Rogen that the movement of the sun — time itself — worked in our favor. The tyrant falls, not because he is too weak, but because he is too strong; each injustice that seemingly strengthens his position, actually hastens his downfall. The dead body of Bjorn was more dangerous to Sigurd than Bjorn alive would have been. It was a symbol to the weak and the downtrodden, and when they would begin to fear for their own lives, their very cowardice would lead them to perform deeds that a brave man would never stoop to.

The tyrant lives in fear of poison, the knife in the shadow, and the witch's brew. The brave and the just know their enemies as well as they know their friends. The tyrant can only guess at the fear that lives in the hearts of his subjects and, by ever increasing it, hope to escape their vengeance.

Harold the Bowbender had told me that he would come to the cave with Rark when the sun had sunk into the sea for the fourth time after our meeting. During these four days I stayed in the cave and Trold was a great comfort to me. I imagined poor Helga walking the mountainside looking for me, probably not knowing herself that she was a bait in Eirik the Fox's trap. I kept repeating to myself, "Harold will protect her." But I did not dare ask myself how.

It was Trold's growl that told me of the arrival of Harold and Rark. I had retreated to the back of the big cave; while at the entrance I had built a fire, so that I could see anyone who might enter without being seen myself.

"Hakon!" Rark called.

I ran from my hiding place to embrace my friend. Rark was smiling and his eyes were moist. Tears are funny guests, as fond of arriving when you are happy as when you are unhappy. Harold's news was better than I had hoped for. For two days Eirik and his men had followed little Helga as she scoured the northern and eastern sides of the Mountain of the Sun. The steeper western and southern faces of the mountain she had avoided, complaining that they were too difficult to climb.

When we heard this, Rark and I nodded our heads in amazement and admiration. Helga must have guessed Eirik the Fox's plot, and suspected that I might be hiding in the same cave to which Rark had taken her, when Ulv Erikson was hunting them.

Poor Helga was tired, but no one hurt her. My uncle himself called off the search for me, and declared me dead. My birthright he claimed for his own eldest son. Few believed my uncle's assertion, and seven of the best warriors on Rogen told Harold the Bowbender that, if I were alive, they would come to my aid as soon as I unfurled my banner. My old plan of escaping by boat was now discarded, and a new plan was formed — the retaking of Rogen.

It would have been best for us if we could have waited — at least as long as it takes the moon to wane and grow full again — but we did not dare. Eirik the Fox had a sharp nose and a coward's heart. He was trying to convince my uncle to ban Harold and four other men from the island. They were to be given a small boat and enough food to reach the mainland. In this way Eirik hoped to get rid of his most troublesome subjects without creating new enemies. Apparently none but Rark and myself needed to fear for his life, for Eirik and my uncle had finally realized how much hate the murdering of freemen aroused.

I thought it best that Rark should stay with me, but he refused, explaining that his escape might spoil our plot. We had decided that we would attack Eirik's hall on the first night of the dark moon. We were to meet at sunset, by those rocks which Eirik hid behind when he shot an arrow at me.

It was sad to say goodbye to my friends, for, though my dog Trold was good company, I missed the sound of human voices. Once they had left I returned to my own cave — the smaller one — to sleep, but I could not rest. Dreams and reality turned in my head as if I had a fever. I walked down to the beach and threw sticks into the water for Trold to retrieve — a game he never tired of.

15

A PLAN should be whole and tight like a cooking pot, and ours seemed to me to resemble a fishing net. Ifs and ifs piled on top of each other make a poor house, but luck always favors the young.

The day following our meeting I stayed in the cave. By night I grew restless and decided to test my luck by hunting. I took my bow and arrows, and walked in the direction of Eirik's hall.

A half moon shone in the light summer sky. I saw no one by the houses, but I dared not go too near. About ten spear-lengths from the main hall, I hid behind a bush. In the pale twilight the houses looked filled with mystery, more as if they were the habitations of elves or trolls than of human beings. The door to the hall opened. A man stepped out and glanced with sleepy eyes up toward the sky. It was Eirik the Fox!

Without thinking, I put an arrow on my bow-string, pulled it back, and with my full strength let the arrow fly. It stuck in the door, a little above Eirik's shoulder. He turned in my direction, and I saw the shock and terror in his expression before he fled to safety inside. I sprang up and ran back towards the Mountain of the Sun.

All that night and the next day I worried about my foolish deed. Harold had told me to stay in the cave, so that no one would see me. And what about Rark? Would the arrow that missed Eirik be his death? A man that is governed by his temper is a fool: a piece of driftwood that is at the mercy of the currents and cannot steer its own course.

When the sun rose for the second time after my foolish attempt to kill Eirik the Fox, I could no longer stand being confined in the cave. To my conscience I used the excuse that I had no more food. I climbed to the top of the mountain. From there I could see the big hall, and as I stood there watching it, I dreamed that it was still my father's house and that he still lived there.

Suddenly I saw, far below me, an army of men — probably all of the men on Rogen — walking towards the Mountain of the Sun. I knew that they had come to hunt, and I knew the name of the hare — Hakon Long-ears!

I hurried back to the cave and put out the fire; I feared that the smoke might be detected. I waited long, my arm around Trold's neck. At last I heard people calling to each other and I feared that the dog might bark. But Trold seemed to understand his master's danger, and with that sorrow mirrored in his eyes that only animals seem to know, he looked up at me. I climbed over the hearth, with Trold following, and in through the tunnel. The narrow passage held no fear for me any more, and soon I was in the big cave. Squatting by the opening of the tunnel, in the recesses of the cave, I waited — for what I wasn't sure.

My legs fell asleep and I stretched them in order to make myself more comfortable. Time passed slowly. Trold kept trying to lick my face, and I — in order to avoid his wet kisses — scratched his ears.

I was just about to return to the smaller cave when something moved at the entrance. I felt all the muscles in Trold's body stiffen, and the hair on his neck rose.

"Why should he be there? We are wasting our time. I think Eirik dreamed that arrow." The voice of Harold the Bowbender was very loud, and I guessed that he had spoken to warn me.

"You can't dream an arrow!" Eirik returned irritably.

"Have you so few enemies that no one but that boy should wish you dead?" The shock of hearing my uncle speak made me tremble.

"Olaf, go inside the cave," Eirik commanded.

Olaf, who was called Olaf the Toothless for he had lost his front teeth in a fight, replied, "Go yourself, Eirik!" Olaf was quarrelsome; everyone knew that he had no liking for the dark.

"Olaf the Brave!" my uncle said sarcastically.

"And do you know where the cave leads to? Who knows what spirits live in its darkness!" Olaf's voice was shaking, partly from anger, partly from fear.

"Eirik, why don't you go. You are a brave man."

I did not recognize the voice, but its tone must have made Eirik wince, and he made a noise as an animal does when it feels itself being menaced.

"I will go." It was Harold who had spoken, and I drew a sigh of relief, for even though I might manage to escape — by crawling through the tunnel into the smaller cave — the ashes from my fire would make anyone who saw it ever suspect that this was my dwelling place.

"No, Harold, Eirik will go." My uncle's tone was commanding, not asking.

I saw Eirik very plainly when he entered, then he was lost in the shadows. "It is very big." The tremor in his voice indicated that he would have preferred the cave to have been small.

"Walk to the very bottom of it," my uncle demanded very sternly from without.

I could judge from his footfalls that Eirik was moving very slowly towards the middle of the cave. At that moment when he had gained the very center, Trold — who had been so quiet that I had forgotten him — howled. A long, low groan, that echoed throughout the cave, and sounded like the wailings of the spirits in Hades. A scream of terror answered Trold's howl.

I did not wait to hear what effect this had had on my pursuers. I pushed Trold in front of me into the tunnel, and I returned to the little cave.

Later I was told by Harold the Bowbender that, when Eirik came out of the cave, he was so frightened he was speechless. When they returned to Sigurd's hall and Eirik was able to talk, he insisted that he had seen the Fenris Wolf — its eyes as big as shields and burning like fires. Like the fool he was, he kept repeating the story, and by that gained many converts for my cause.

The people whispered that the gods had taken pity upon the orphan, and it was said that the Fenris Wolf suckled me to keep me from starving. Harold and Rark were quick to take advantage of these rumors to further my cause. They claimed that the reason I had not been found was that the mountain itself had hidden the unjustly treated son of Olaf the Lame.

16

THE SEA swallowed up the sun, and the white night came. I left my cave and, followed by Trold, made my way to Eirik's hall. By now, during the darkest part of the night, the fainter of the stars were visible.

Hiding behind a bush, I watched the hall. All was still — an owl hooted and I trembled. A strange bird, the owl, with its huge eyes, neckless body, and great fear of the sunlight. We had few owls on Rogen, and some of the old people were fond of finding omens in their nightly cry. Many believed that if an owl sat on a house someone within must die before the moon was full. During that year every house on Rogen should have had a dozen owls on its rooftop, to hoot their miserable messages. Why are there so many bad omens, and so few good ones? Why does man find so much pleasure in foretelling future calamities, and so little in his present happiness? Even at a wedding feast, when bride and groom with eyes shining like bright stars sit at table, the guests are ever fond — while sighing from their well-filled stomachs — of speaking of omens of ill-will. The bird will sing when hunger's hand is on its throat, but kings, above their golden horns of mead, will speak only of envy, fear, and hate.

I passed Eirik's hall, and made my way towards my uncle's. The owl followed me, hooting its warning to the world. The night was growing whiter and the eastern sky was red as blood.

The animal in hiding — even the hare whose heart ever beats in fear — has moments when a strange courage takes possession of it, and utterly changes its nature. So it was with me. I walked without fear among the buildings, hardly caring whether I was seen or not.

From the pigpen I heard moans. I opened its low doors and looked in. There lay Rark, his wrists and ankles tied together like a sheep who is about to be butchered.

Quickly I cut the ropes that bound him, but they had been pulled so tightly that Rark's feet and hands were numb and useless. He tried to stand up, but he could only with difficulty get to his knees. I dragged him outside; his face was swollen from a beating my uncle had given him, and he had had nothing to eat for three days. I laid him on the ground by that wall of the pigpen that was farthest from the hall, and went in search of a horse.

My father's old mare was grazing in the meadow, and I ran up to her, hoping that she would play no tricks on me. She was liable to let one chase her for a long time before she would consent to be caught. As if she understood the seriousness of the situation, she stood perfectly still when I came up to her, only turning her head to stare with her big brown eyes at my face. I slipped the halter, which I had found in the stable, over her head, and rode her back to where Rark was lying.

In my haste I had not taken a saddle, and it was difficult to get Rark up on the mare's back, but at last I succeeded. Skirting the buildings, I led the horse across the meadow, then I gave the halter to Rark and told him to ride on. He was much too weak and confused to protest. He only nodded his head to tell me that he had understood.

I returned to the buildings. Everything was still and deserted. I sneaked into the hen house and grabbed one of the sleeping hens. Before it had time to make any noise, I killed it; two more I slew in the same manner, but the fourth flew out of my hands. I ran out of the hen house, expecting that the clucking of the hens would awaken one of the men.

Fortunately for me, during the past few days great schools of fish had been sighted near Rogen, and the men had been almost continuously at sea. Now they were tired and they slept on. From the women I had nothing to fear. It was rare that any of them would rouse herself to investigate a noise. On the whole they worked longer and harder than the men, and would not take on a task which was not normally held to be theirs.

I followed the edge of the forest and ran south, grinning to myself at the thought of my uncle's expression — some hours hence — when he would discover that his prisoner had escaped, and that the cock in his hen-yard was missing a few of his wives.

I caught up with Rark a little southwest of Eirik's hall, and slinging the hens, whose legs I had tied together, over the mare's back, I took the bridle-lead.

As we came nearer the Mountain of the Sun, it became increasingly difficult for the mare to find foothold among the boulders. Finally we had to give up. Rark lowered himself down from her back, and found that his legs — though weak — could support him. I jumped on the mare's back and rode it to where the boulders stopped. There I took off the bridle, gave the mare a slap on her flanks and watched her trot homeward.

When I returned to Rark, he was sitting rubbing his ankles. Looking up at me, he said, "Thank you." It embarrasses a fool to give thanks and a wise man to receive them. Though Rark was no fool, I was not wise, so I basked in the fact of having saved my friend's life, like a seal sunning himself on a rock.

With great difficulty and much pain, Rark made his way to the small cave. I threw wood on the fire, and while I plucked one of the hens, Rark told me news of home.

"The day after Harold and I visited you, I was locked in the little storehouse. Your uncle knows very well that I hate him, and he suspects that I might be plotting against him, but his greed prevented him from killing me. Each time he looked at me, he saw not only me, but the pile of silver a slave is worth — alive! Several people visited me. Erik the Poet came and sat on the floor in silence, his brow furrowed in concentration over the work of forming his thoughts into words. I really thought that he would never speak, and I was not surprised when he rose — as if he were about to go — without having said anything. But at the door he turned and remarked haltingly, 'I am for Hakon . . .' Funny man, Erik. He is not stupid, but language is a tool he cannot use."

I had finished plucking the hen. Now I cut it open and removed the entrails which I gave to Trold. I was very pleased that Erik the Poet was on my side. As a child I had often played tricks on him — not all of them kind or innocent.

"Erik Longbeard came too. He is a good man to have join us, but I wish he were not so vain about that beard of his," Rark continued. "All the time that he and I were talking, he sat combing his beard or pulling gently at it. Olaf the Toothless came. He said he despised both your uncle and Eirik the Fox, and wanted only to see you get your inheritance back."

I had put the hen into the earthen pot, and it was now boiling away over the fire. "Did you believe Olaf the Toothless?" I asked.

Rark laughed. "Believe him? I would never believe anything Olaf said. If I woke from sleep and Olaf said it was night, I would stick my head outside to make certain. But even a liar will tell the truth sometimes. I believe that Olaf was sent by your uncle, but it is possible that he came by himself because he was afraid. Naturally, I told him that I was a miserable slave, who had no opinion but my master's, and no master but Sigurd Sigurdson."

Rark inhaled deeply. "That chicken smells like the food of heaven."

I knew that Rark belonged to the new religion. He was fond of placing the people he liked in heaven, and the ones he disliked in Hades. Thora had also believed in the new religion, but she believed that only heaven existed and that Hades was here on earth. Her religion had been an inner part of her. It left her naked and vulnerable, and yet, protected her. Rark's religion was a coarse piece of clothing that kept him warm, and he offered it only so much attention as he thought necessary. If it was torn, he mended it. When summer came, he put it away and never gave it a thought until the fall storms again began to howl.

"How did you end up in the pigpen?"

Rark was leaning his head close to the pot, breathing in the vapors from the chicken soup.

"I had too many visitors in the storehouse."

"And the beating?"

"Don't you think it might be finished — the hen, I mean?"

"Because of me!" I insisted. "Because my uncle wanted to find out from you where I was."

Rark looked at me with embarrassment. "It is three days since I last ate," he muttered.

I took the pot off the fire, stuck my knife into the hen, and lifted it out of the soup.

17

AFTER Rark's escape, would any of our friends be safe? I had made an agreement with Harold the Bowbender that should I think it necessary to call upon him and the other men who were willing to fight for my cause before the dark of the moon (the night we had planned for the attack), I would build a bonfire on the northern slope of the Mountain of the Sun, at a point where it would be visible to the whole island.

The day after Rark's escape we collected wood for the bonfire, and as soon as the sun was low in the horizon, we set it ablaze. The wood was summer-dry, and soon the flames rose thrice a man's height into the sky.

Quickly we returned to the cave to await Harold the Bowbender. A sheep I had stolen that very morning was being roasted over a fire. As I stared into the flames, I asked myself how many would come? Would there be enough warriors to win a battle, or only just enough for a heroic defeat?

A few minutes after midnight the first arrivals came: Erik Longbeard and Erik the Poet, and a young man only two years older than myself, Hakon the Black, whose hair was the color of a raven's wing. These men were from my uncle's hall. Erik Longbeard noticed that I was disappointed, and assured me that two others were coming: Thor the Lame and Magnus One-Ear, who were out with the sheep. Both of these men were old warriors, but if their age made them of less value in battle, their wisdom in counsel made up for it. Erik Longbeard offered to go and look for them.

While Erik the Poet and Hakon the Black each carved himself a hunk of roasted lamb and started to eat, I walked outside. The night was clear. A gentle breeze blew from the southwest. I decided to attend my bonfire. I didn't want its message to die down like a cry for help, strangled by fear. I wanted the flames to shout defiance at my uncle and Eirik the Fox.

Soon it would be decided who was to be master of Rogen. When I was a child, I drank the tales of valor as a babe suckles its mother's milk, but those tales had neither fear, nor pain, nor death in them. They resembled reality in the same way that the boats we — as children — made of bark, resembled the big fifty-oar ships that can brave the northern storms.

The fire had burned down. Low flames flittered across the blackened wood. I collected several dry branches and threw them on the embers. It crackled like a thousand twigs being snapped at once, and I felt the heat of the flames as they leaped skyward. I did not think that any of the enemy could be near; still it was not wise to stand too close to the flames and make a target of one's self. Each time I put another piece of wood on the fire, I dived quickly back into the shadows. When the fire again was burning brightly, I decided to return to the cave.

I did not see the man coming up the mountain before he was quite near. It was lucky for me that it was a friend, for he approached so close to me, that he could have killed me before I had a glimpse of him.

"Shall we call you Hakon the Fearless or Hakon the Fool?" The speaker was Magnus the Fair, a tall blond man, with a sharp tongue, who had often irritated my father.

"An ill-fitting name, Magnus, is as bothersome as an ill-fitting cloak. Have you come to swear allegiance to me?"

"I have come to unswear my allegiance to your uncle. Will that do?" Whenever Magnus spoke he smiled, in this way making certain that no one ever knew his opinion. Magnus the Fair was a good warrior, and honored for his strength as much as he was feared for his tongue.

"The man who swims with the tide is of little use to me." This was not really true, but my feelings were hurt because he had not said that he would swear his allegiance to me.

"And those who swim only against the currents are fools and of no use to anyone."

The smile lurking in the corner of his mouth made me peevishly angry. "How do you know that the tide will turn? How do you know that my uncle won't remain master of Rogen?"

Magnus thought a moment, then, with a broad grin, he answered. "Your uncle's friends are bound to him not by friendship, but by common crimes. That kind of comradeship is a leaky vessel in a storm. Still, they will not give up without a battle, and who knows who will live to swear allegiance to whom. Hakon the Orphan may yet go to his father's hall, without ever having sat in his father's seat."

I was annoyed. I gave my trust so willingly — even carelessly — to those whom I loved and claimed to love me, that I had yet to learn that common advantage is a string in the ruler's bow.

While we talked, we had been walking in the direction of the cave. Outside the entrance sat Harold the Bowbender. When he saw me coming he stood up.

"How many men have you brought me, Harold?" I asked and, fearing the answer, I said to myself, "No less than six! By the gods, no less than six!"

"Eight, including myself."

"Half of Eirik's men! Oh, that fox has a short tail now!" In my happiness I embraced Harold, who goodnaturedly laughed at me and stroked my hair.

"You have more than half his men. He has to count on Olaf the Toothless, Sven the Dane, Erling the Swift, Ragnvald Harelip, and Thorstein the Old. We all know what kind of man Olaf the Toothless is. And Sven, Erling, Ragnvald, and Thorstein are the ones who fled from the battle on Thor's Mountain, when your father was slain."

"If they were cowards then, will they not be cowards again, and betray your uncle as they did your father?" Magnus commented softly.

"What if I pardoned them their betrayal of my father? Wouldn't they welcome an excuse not to have to fight at all?"

Harold the Bowbender answered pensively, "Eirik the Fox has told them that you mean to avenge yourself upon them, and that if you win, you will offer them to Odin."

I shook my head. I could not understand how anyone could believe that I was capable of doing anything so cruel.

"Come," Harold said, "let me present you to my comrades."

Harold's comrades were the very best men on the island: his sons, Nils and Eigil, Erp the Traveler, Giermund the Handsome, Frode the Peaceful, Halfdan the Carver, and Ketil Ragnvaldson. At Ketil I looked long and searchingly, for his father was Ragnvald Harelip who had chosen to stand by Eirik the Fox. Ketil became uncomfortable under my scrutiny and blushed.

"A son's crime may make white a father's hair, and a father's deeds give red cheeks to his son's face."

I extended my hand to Ketil. "Each man's life is his own, and none but his own deeds shall speak for him. You are welcome, Ketil Ragnvaldson." Ketil grabbed my hand and pressed it.

"Do you all swear allegiance to Hakon Olafson, to help him regain his father's hall and his father's seat as Chieftain of Rogen?"

As Harold the Bowbender spoke, I looked at all the faces that were turned towards me, and momentarily a fear of not being able to speak overcame me.

"By Odin's raven that hears all, by Thor's hammer that no man can escape, I swear it!" Magnus One-Ear proclaimed. He was standing near the fire, and his white beard had turned red in the light from the flames.

"We swear!" the others growled, like angry wolves.

"You have sworn to be loyal to me. Let me swear, as well, that I will be loyal to you." My voice broke at that moment, and became a child's voice. I paused to get control of it, so that I could speak with deeper tones. "I swear that on Rogen shall rule only justice. That no man shall fear his tongue nor his thought, but each man shall live in peace."

After my speech there was silence, which was finally broken by Magnus the Fair: "I will swear my allegiance to Hakon Olafson, but remember that an oath by Odin and Thor has been broken before. Keep your own promise as a guiding star and you will never need to ask anyone for his loyalty."

The words that Magnus spoke were true, but I wished that they had come from another's mouth — one that was not twisted in a smile. Was it because of vanity that Magnus could never hide his contempt of others? Or was it a kind of wisdom which ever will isolate and make lonely the man who possesses it?

The sun had just risen above the horizon, when Harold called for a discussion of plans. Thor and Einer were in favor of staying on the mountain, to give others a chance to join our side. Nils and Eigil Haroldson wanted to attack immediately. Most of the rest were undecided, for Harold the Bowbender had not spoken yet.

Rark stood close by me, but could not offer his opinion, for he knew that there were a few of the men who would close their ears to his voice because of their contempt for a slave. He leaned close to me and whispered in a fierce and unhappy tone, "Hakon, we must attack now, for Helga's sake. She is in Eirik's house."

I had forgotten my little sister, my playfellow, and I felt guilty for I knew that I dared not explain to the others my reason for wanting to attack at once. For a slave woman's daughter, freemen could not be asked to go into battle. "We have not food enough here," I argued instead, "nor weapons. Each tiny movement of the sun in the heaven will aid my uncle. Eirik the Fox is fearridden now. Let us give him no time to gather courage."

The young men were on my side, but several of the older hoped that if we waited my uncle might be forced to give up without a battle.

"Hakon is right." At last Harold had spoken and with a sigh of relief, I realized that the old men would not dare to oppose him. "We will visit Eirik the Fox first. Have we a hall to live in and food to eat, our voices will be stronger, and who knows how big a flock Sigurd Sigurdson will have tomorrow. As long as we are like wolves in the forest, only the brave will join us, but once we sit at our own table, men will flock to take their place on our benches."

So it was decided. In a long file, Eirik the Fox's uninvited guests left the mountain. Harold the Bowbender and I walked in front. Harold was singing a song, and I was walking beside him, my heart swollen with pride.

18

As we approached Eirik the Fox's hall, we spread out in a half-circle. An arrow's shot from the buildings, we halted. A few chickens walked in the cabbage patch, busily examining the earth for food; otherwise, the place looked deserted.

"They have gone!" I exclaimed and stared with dread at the peaceful buildings, for I feared that we would find tragedy inside.

"It could be a trap," Harold muttered. He stuck his spear into the ground, unsheathed his sword, and walked towards the buildings. I started to follow him but he ordered me to stay behind.

We watched him. Without knowing it, each of us took a step forward as his figure disappeared around the corner of the hall. We waited a few moments, advanced a few steps, and stopped. Each man had an arrow on his bowstring, and our beating hearts gave the lie to the calm hands on our weapons. Harold reappeared. On his face was a wide grin, and he beckoned us toward him. With cries of joy, the men ran forward, but a fear in my heart for little Helga closed my lips.

The place was deserted. In their joy at so easy a victory, most of the men did not realize that something was wrong — where were the women and children? Harold the Bowbender was a widower, and his two sons unmarried as yet. But both Erp and Giermund had wives and children, and Halfdan, a mother. That Ketil's mother had gone with his father, Ragnvald was not surprised; but where was Frode's little girl, whose birth had cost his wife's life?

No one understood what had happened. The men started to search the buildings. In one of the storehouses, we found Freya the Old. She was a woman so ancient that no one knew her age. Many of the more foolish among the people of Rogen feared her, and said

she was a witch. The truth was that she had reached that age when memory leaves, and takes with it wisdom.

Poor Freya had hidden herself, for she was not yet so childish that she did not understand the importance of the message she had been left behind to give us. Brought out into daylight, and surrounded by the angry men, fear made her silent. Magnus the Fair, who knew her best, took her aside and comforted her, drawing the story of Eirik's departure from her, word by word.

Everyone had taken for granted that in a fight between kinsmen, women and children were left unharmed. So much had they trusted in this tradition, that they had left their most precious possessions to their enemies. When they now were told that Eirik had taken their wives and children as hostages, their hatred became so violent that, had Eirik been among them, not even the god Odin could have saved his life.

It was decided to send Thor the Lame to my uncle to demand the immediate return of the hostages. Before he left I asked him to see if Helga was at my uncle's. I did not dare demand her return, thinking that, for her own sake, it would be better to act as if her fate did not concern me.

At evening Thor the Lame returned; the women were with him, but not the children. It was a fox-smelling plot that Thor had to report to us. My uncle offered me half the island and Eirik's hall, if I would acknowledge him and his sons as the rulers of Rogen. I was to take my uncle's old position, and he, my father's seat, and his sons, my birthright. If we did not agree to this, he would kill the children one by one, beginning with the slave girl Helga — "Of whom," he had said, "my nephew seems to be so fond."

My uncle had only given us until the next day at noon, to reach our decision, so we held counsel at once. Had my uncle not been so clever as to return the women to their husbands, there would have been no discussion. Women care little for honor and much for their children, but only a fool would judge them ill for that.

As the men and women filed into the hall, I lingered outside, wanting a word with Harold the Bowbender. He guessed my intentions and joined me. "Well, Hakon, and what do you say to Sigurd's message?"

I did not know what to answer and stood silent.

"Will you agree?"

"The right to rule Rogen is not so valuable a prize that I would sacrifice a child's life for it," I finally said.

Harold smiled sarcastically, and for a moment his face reminded me of Magnus the Fair's. I realized that Harold did not believe me, and I wished myself back in my cave, alone.

"But one cannot trust my uncle's word." While I spoke, I looked at my feet, thinking all the time, "This will be your excuse."

"So you don't want to give Rogen to Sigurd?"

"No!" I shouted with such passion, as though the word had grown in my body and had become bigger than it, and therefore needed to escape.

"Good!" Harold touched my shoulder. "Sigurd

118

Sigurdson is not worthy of being the ruler of the gulls on Grass Island."

"But the children!"

"We will give him no time to hurt them. We will attack tonight."

"But will everyone agree?" I nodded towards the hall.

Harold thought for a moment, then he said, "I don't want *everyone*."

Quickly he told me his plans, and we entered the hall together. Everyone looked at us, trying to guess from our faces what we had decided. I seated myself in Eirik the Fox's big, heavy chair at the head of the table. Harold placed himself at the end of the bench on my right.

"I have decided, for the sake of the children, whose innocent blood I do not want on my hands, to agree to my uncle's demands."

Most of the men were shocked, the women were relieved, and on Thor the Lame's face I thought I saw a sneer.

Eigil Haroldson sprang to his feet and shouted at me, "Hakon the Orphan shall soon be Hakon the Friendless!" And then — since I did not reply — he ran from the hall, banging the door behind him.

I kept my temper, and followed Harold the Bow-bender's advice, which was to send Einer One-Ear and Thor the Lame to my uncle with the message that we would agree to his terms. Harold wanted both of these men to go, for he trusted neither of them and suspected that they were spies.

For sentries, Harold chose men whom we were sure we could trust. The rest of the warriors were told that they could sleep, though none were allowed to undress, and all had to keep their weapons within reach. Also, I lay down to sleep — this was part of our plan, for we wanted to ensure secrecy.

As I lay waiting for the men to fall asleep, time seemed to stand still, as it does on the night before a feast day. Patience is the gift of age, and I had as yet received none of it. On tiptoe I sneaked from the hall, stopping first by Rark's sleeping place to awaken him. But to my surprise, it was empty.

Down by the boats, the warriors whom Harold the Bowbender had selected were gathered: Ketil Ragnvaldson, Magnus the Fair, Hakon the Black, Erik the Poet, and Eigil Haroldson. Nils and Harold himself were not there, nor did I see Rark.

Eigil grabbed my hand and said, "I am sorry, Hakon, for my words in the hall."

I smiled. "But you didn't know our plan."

"But I should have known that a son of Olaf Sigurdson would not give away his birthright."

I remembered Harold's face when I had said that the right to rule Rogen was not as valuable as a child's life. And I realized that if you give away your gold rings or your best cloak, you will gain fame for your generosity, but if you give up power, you will be rewarded with contempt.

The men were in good spirit. They were sure of victory, though they were outnumbered; for none believed that any of Sigurd's men would fight for him.

"Only Eirik the Fox, Sigurd himself, and Sven the Dane will fight. And Eirik will only fight because Rogen is an island and he can't run away," declared Magnus the Fair.

"And why," asked Hakon the Black, "do you think Sven will fight?"

"Sven is a braggart, and his sword is for sale, but he knows that with the blood that is already on it, no man on Rogen but Sigurd will buy it."

I sat down upon the beach and waited for Harold's return. Soon we saw his figure come striding towards us; he carried himself with the agility of a youth, in spite of his forty-two winters.

Harold looked searchingly about him, as though someone were missing. "Where is Rark?" he asked me, and I told him that Rark was not in the hall and that I did not know where he was. "By Thor, I think I know! We'd better hurry."

Quickly he gave orders to the others: Magnus and Hakon the Black were to approach the enemy from the beach; Eigil, Ketil, and Erik the Poet were to bypass the hall and attack from the north; Harold, Nils, and I would come up from the south. Any sentries we came upon were to be wounded, rather than killed — preferably stunned by a blow with the flat of the sword.

"Are you afraid?" Harold asked me looking into my eyes.

"A little," I answered.

"Good." He laughed. "You will make a chieftain yet. If something should go wrong . . . remember my sons. They will serve you well, if you will serve them."

I nodded my head. "Chieftain," I thought, and then a little bitterly, "who is chieftain here but Harold?"

Looking up at him, walking beside me, his body relaxed, his face serene, and yet his eyes sparkling with life, I felt ashamed of myself for having such thoughts.

19

WHEN Harold and I came within sight of my uncle's hall, we halted behind some shrubbery. Until now we had seen no guards, but we soon saw that there could be no thought of taking the place by surprise, for my uncle had posted sentries.

We were waiting for Nils Haroldson, and Harold was obviously worried for he had been expecting his son to meet us before now. An owl hooted further inland. Harold put his hands to his mouth, and imitating an owl, he hooted three times. Immediately, the other owl repeated the message. We crawled on our bellies in the direction that the hoot of the owl had come from. Behind a small clump of trees we found Nils.

He told us that Sigurd had not posted sentries by the buildings that faced north (perhaps because he wasn't expecting an attack from that direction, and probably he had too few men that he could trust). We decided to send Nils to get Magnus and Hakon the Black, who were hiding near the beach. They came quickly. Then we all made our way to the forest, and from there, north. When we were certain that we had walked far enough north to have passed the hall, we turned east, towards the coast. Here we joined Erik the Poet, Eigil, and

Ketil Ragnvaldson, and together we started towards the hall.

The northern approach offered the further advantage that a series of small hills made excellent hiding places. From the crest of the one nearest the hall, we had a good view of all the buildings; Nils was right — there were no sentries on this side.

"I wonder where the children are," I whispered to Harold. He nodded but said nothing. "We ought to know that first, before we attack." Again Harold nodded his head; then he motioned with his hands for us to retreat from the ridge of the hill.

Huddled together at the bottom of the hill, we held counsel. Ketil Ragnvaldson was for attacking right away, but Harold overruled him. Harold had decided that he alone would approach the buildings, and try to discover which one housed the children. His plan was that we should take that house first.

Again we crawled to the crest of the hill, and again we ascertained that there were no sentries that might warn my uncle of our coming. Then Harold climbed down the other side of the hill. We watched him. He was crawling on all fours, taking advantage of each rock, little incline, and bush to arrive unseen.

When Harold had reached the first of the buildings, a small hut used for the hens, I could not bear lying still and useless any longer. Turning to Nils, who lay beside me, I said, "Wait here!" and plunged over the top of the hill. I heard Nils whisper, "No," but I paid no attention. With my sword drawn, I followed Harold, imitating his approach. I did not look back until

I arrived at the hen house. It was only then that I saw that Ketil, Nils, and Eigil had followed me. For better or worse, the attack had started!

Bent over, as if a crooked back could make me invisible, I ran round the corner of the house. In front of me, crouching behind a low stone wall that formed the fence of the pigpen, I saw Harold. Silently I made my way to him, and crouched by his side. He looked at me with a little smile, but he said nothing. A big sow came close to our hiding place and grunted loudly. Harold took advantage of this to whisper to me, "Are the others coming?"

"Yes."

Harold leaned his head close to my ear and said, "Tell them to wait by the hen house."

I returned to the hen house. Ketil was already there, and soon the last of our band, Erik the Poet, arrived. I gave them Harold's instructions, and then ran back to tell him that we were all there. When I regained the wall of the pigsty, Harold was gone. On all fours, I made my way around the corner to find him. He was standing by the western wall of the big storehouse, and I was about to join him when I saw another figure approaching from the northern side. It was Eirik the Fox!

When Eirik saw Harold, he drew his sword from his belt. As we had seen no sentries, Harold was not expecting an attack from behind. I did not give myself time to warn Harold, but rushed with my sword drawn towards Eirik. He was so occupied with the thought of the easy victory he would have over Harold the Bowbender, that he did not hear me before I was only a few steps away from him. As he was about to raise his sword, he was pierced by mine. With a loud scream, he fell to the ground.

Harold turned and looked with astonishment at the dying man, lying so close to him. I pulled out the sword. The sight of the blood made me sick. Oh, why does man have a lamb's tongue and a wolf's teeth?

At the death cry of Eirik our comrades came running. Seeing my bloody sword and Eirik's dead body, they gave a cry of triumph.

With their yelling the need for secrecy was gone; now the more noise we made the better. We rushed first for the hall, hoping to capture my uncle, and thus end the battle. But my uncle was not there. The hall was filled with women and children. Seeing them, I called loudly, "Helga! Helga!"

No one answered me. Among the women I saw my aunt, and I ran up to her. She — seeing my bloody sword — believed that I had come to kill her, and drew her children close to her and shrieked again and again. Close by her sat Ragnhild, Eirik the Fox's wife. Pointing my sword at her, I shouted, "Where is Helga?"

Staring with fear-filled eyes at my weapon, dirty with her husband's blood, whom she did not know was dead, she replied, "Sigurd took her with him." She said no more, but nodded towards the back of the hall, where a small door led to the outside. I ran to the door and threw it open.

Sven the Dane with a spear in hand stood guard on the other side. With my sword, I hit his spear so hard that the wooden shaft broke in two, and Sven looked with amazement at the little piece of wood in his hand. Then throwing it aside, he fled.

I do not know why I ran towards the beach, for in my state, I was not capable of thinking clearly. The cove where the big boats were lying was deserted. I swung my sword in the air and screamed, "Sigurd Sigurdson!" Only a gull answered me, but along the coast, running in the direction of the other hall (the one which my uncle had given to Eirik the Fox, and later offered to me) I saw two figures: a tall man with a sword in one hand, who was dragging a child with the other.

"Sigurd!" I screamed, "touch her and you die!"

He was too far away; he could not hear me. I could not understand why he was fleeing in the direction of Eirik's hall, until I realized that there were not two but three persons: my uncle had a pursuer. An arrow's shot behind him, and gaining fast, came Rark!

My uncle stumbled, but then his foot found hold again. Ahead of him was a beach, and beyond that the place where the boats were drawn up — the very place where Harold the Bowbender had first sworn his loyalty to me. With panic, I remembered that the smallest boat was usually anchored by a rock in the water. If Sigurd reached that he might escape taking little Helga with him.

All of this I thought, while I ran as fast as I could to catch up with Rark. Here the coast was not sandy, but made of stones that had been worn round by the surf, and many a time I fell. Once I bruised my knee so badly that it bled.

Near the point where the sandy beach began, a cliff jutted out into the sea, and for the moment I lost sight of the others. When I climbed to the top of it, I could see that Rark was but a spear's length behind my uncle.

Sigurd let go of Helga and she fell face down upon the sand. Rark stopped and reached for the girl, while I screamed with my full force, "Look out, Rark!" For my uncle instead of continuing to flee, had turned around, and was now rushing with raised sword at Rark and Helga.

Rark heard my cry. From his half-reclining position — one knee resting on the sand — he managed with his own sword to deflect the blade of my uncle's, so that it hit not his head — for which it had been aimed — but his left shoulder.

My uncle drew back. Rark was on his feet. I could see the blood rushing from his wound. Then I jumped down from the cliff to the sand beach. As I ran, it felt as if my heart were no longer in my breast but beating in my throat. Before me I saw the two fighting men, and beneath me, the wet sand of the beach. Then all of a sudden I stood still.

The fight was over. I saw my uncle's sword fall from his hand and the ugly gaping wound in his neck. Sigurd's face wore that same look of surprise that I had seen on Bjorn's face, when my uncle had slain him.

Rark turned towards Helga, but his legs gave way under him and he fell. Quickly, I ran to his side. His wound was clean and deep. I looked for something to bandage it with. My own clothes were of too rough a wool to be used. My uncle was wearing his fine linen

shirt, the one which he had bought a few years before in Tronhjem. It was made from a material that comes from the countries far to the south of Norway. I slit it, and tore it from my uncle's body.

Helga stood nearby, frightened and trembling. Forgetting everything she had gone through, I told her sharply to go to Eirik's hall for help. She stared at me unbelievingly, and started to cry. Then I realized that she probably didn't know that now she would find only friends at that hall. As hurriedly as I could, I explained to her that she was no longer in peril, but that Rark's life would depend upon her swiftness in getting help. She ran away weeping — whether out of fear or relief from it, I shall never know.

I raised Rark's left arm above his head to close the wound and stop the flow of blood, then I bandaged his shoulder.

Eirik Longbeard and Erp the Traveler, sleep still in their eyes, looked at my uncle who was lying face down in the sand, and shook their heads.

We carried Rark to the hall. When the blood-soaked bandage was removed, the wound itself shone at us like the flower of the poppy plant that blooms in the spring. With skillful hand Erp, who was known as a healer, explored the wound; then a new bandage was made, and Rark was placed — sitting up — on one of the benches.

He looked strange: his face pale, his left arm lifted above the bandaged shoulder, his hand resting on top of his head. Erp laughed and said, "Three or four days you must sit like this. But then, that is small payment for the gift of being able to brag that you sent Sigurd Sigurdson to Valhalla!"

Rark said nothing, but I could see on his face that the words had not pleased him. Soon we were alone in the hall, Rark, Helga, and myself. The rest had gone to my father's hall. I heard one man say, "Hakon's hall."

Rark looked at me, and then at Helga. "Never brag of having slain a man, Hakon. Life is holy, and even the foulest of men has once been a child and worthy of love."

Helga was sitting close to me, and my right arm was resting on her shoulder. "I killed Eirik the Fox," I said. To my surprise, the tone of my voice was sad. Helga reached out her hand and touched my forehead, and without knowing why, I thought of my stepmother Thora.

Rark closed his eyes. The loss of blood was making him sleepy. I took Helga's hand in mine. Suddenly her voice echoed in the deserted hall, "You are master of Rogen, Hakon!"

Impatiently, I put my finger to my mouth, to remind her that Rark needed rest.

"You have gotten your birthright back!" she whispered excited, as if — only now — she realized what had happened.

"Birthright," I repeated. But as I thought of Rark's birthright, of Helga's, and of Gunhild's, the word itself seemed to mock me. I will sail Rark back to his own country, and fetch Gunhild from Ulv Hunger's house and give her her freedom. All of sudden, these thoughts

131

were not wishes — dreams — but certainties, for now I was Hakon of Rogen, as my father had been Olaf of Rogen, a chieftain who could forge out of his dreams deeds that poets would sing of.

"Come!" Eagerly I took Helga's hand, and we walked outside. The sun had risen and the crest of Thor Mountain was blood red.

Turning toward it, I said, "By Thor, by my father's memory, I promise that I shall bring back to Rogen Gunhild, who suckled me when I was born, and give her her freedom! By Odin, I swear that I shall take Rark back to his home!" Then searching for words, I added in a tone less defiant, "And to his children."

I looked out over the sea, the path that leads to all adventures; the wind had died and the waters appeared solid like the rock of the mountain. Helga too was looking at the sea; she shuddered and pressed my hand. I turned to her and touched her hair, which was short-cropped in the manner of slave women. "You must let your hair grow."

Helga's eyes were filled with tears.

"Why are you crying, Helga?" I exclaimed, for tears in a woman's eyes fill a man with guilt and shame, and therefore make him angry.

"I am not a slave," Helga said with a slow and wondering voice, and then almost triumphantly she repeated the words: "I am not a slave!"

Suddenly the wind came up. The sea changed, it moved like a giant serpent.

"That is everyone's birthright, his freedom, and the gods have only one message to us, that we must live."

132